My
BlackBerry®
Curve™

Craig James Johnston

que®

800 East 96th Street,
Indianapolis, Indiana 46240 USA

G000146475

My BlackBerry® Curve™

Copyright © 2010 by Que Publishing

ISBN-13: 978-0-7897-4285-8
ISBN-10: 0-7897-4285-3

Library of Congress Cataloging-in-Publication Data:
Johnston, Craig James, 1967-
  My BlackBerry Curve / Craig James Johnston.
    p. cm.
  ISBN 978-0-7897-4285-8
  1. BlackBerry Curve (Smartphone) 2. Smartphones. 3. Pocket computers. I. Title.
  QA76.8.B52J65 2010
  004.1675—dc22

                                                    2009042361

Printed in the United States of America

First Printing: December 2009

Trademarks

Warning and Disclaimer

Bulk Sales

Que Publishing offers excellent discounts on this book when ordered in quantity for bulk purchases or special sales. For more information, please contact

U.S. Corporate and Government Sales
1-800-382-3419
corpsales@pearsontechgroup.com

For sales outside of the U.S., please contact

International Sales
international@pearson.com

ASSOCIATE PUBLISHER
Greg Wiegand

ACQUISITIONS EDITOR
Michelle Newcomb

DEVELOPMENT EDITOR
Kevin Howard

MANAGING EDITOR
Kristy Hart

PROJECT EDITOR
Anne Goebel

COPY EDITORS
Gayle Johnson
San Dee Phillips

INDEXER
Cheryl Lenser

PROOFREADER
Debbie Williams

TECHNICAL EDITOR
Don Schauer

PUBLISHING COORDINATOR
Cindy Teeters

BOOK DESIGNER
Anne Jones

COMPOSITOR
Nonie Ratcliff

Contents at a Glance

Table of Contents

About the Author

Craig James Johnston has been involved with technology since his school days at Glenwood High in Durban, South Africa, when his school was given some Apple II Europluses. From that moment technology captivated him, and he has owned, supported, evangelized, and written about it ever since.

Craig has been involved in designing and supporting large-scale enterprise networks with integrated email and directory services since 1989. Although he has owned many PDAs, Craig was drawn in by the BlackBerry in 2000 and started down the path of supporting it almost exclusively by 2005. He has held many different IT-related positions in his career, ranging from sales support engineer to mobile-engineering an infrastructure with 35,000 BlackBerrys at a large bank.

In addition to designing and supporting mobile computing environments, Craig writes about these topics for *Smartphone and PDA Essentials* magazine and CrackBerry.com, a leading BlackBerry blog. He also cohosts the CrackBerry.com podcast and his own Mobile Computing Authority podcast. He also wrote the book *Professional BlackBerry*.

Craig enjoys high horsepower and high-speed vehicles, and he tries very hard to obey the speed limits while driving them.

Originally from Durban, South Africa, Craig has lived in the United Kingdom, the San Francisco Bay Area, and New Jersey, where he now lives with his wife, Karen, and a couple of cats.

Craig would love to hear from you. Feel free to contact him about your experiences with this book at http://www.MyBlackBerryCurve.info. All comments, suggestions, and feedback are welcome—positive and negative.

Dedication

To those who work tirelessly with loyalty and dedication but who are not recognized because they do not know the art of pretending to like the office bullies.

Acknowledgments

I would like to express my deepest gratitude to the following people on the *My BlackBerry Curve* team, who all worked extremely hard on this book:

Michelle Newcomb, my acquisitions editor, who worked with me to give this project an edge.

Kevin Howard, my development editor, who made sure we stuck to the successful *My* series format.

Don Schauer, my technical editor, who checked through my work to make sure it was accurate, and who also helped enhance it.

Anne Goebel, my project editor, who managed the review process and rushed me the chapters to review.

Gayle Johnson and San Dee Phillips, my copy editors, who checked and re-checked my text and corrected errors.

In addition to the team at Pearson, I must also thank the following people:

Victoria Berry from Research In Motion, who rushed me a BlackBerry Curve 8900 so that I could take all the screen shots.

Amanda Ginther from Waggener Edstrom Worldwide, who got me a BlackBerry Curve 8520 early on so I could include it in the book.

We Want to Hear from You!

As the reader of this book, *you* are our most important critic and commentator. We value your opinion and want to know what we're doing right, what we could do better, what areas you'd like to see us publish in, and any other words of wisdom you're willing to pass our way.

As an associate publisher for Que Publishing, I welcome your comments. You can email or write me directly to let me know what you did or didn't like about this book—as well as what we can do to make our books better.

Please note that I cannot help you with technical problems related to the topic of this book. We do have a User Services group, however, where I will forward specific technical questions related to the book.

When you write, please be sure to include this book's title and author as well as your name, email address, and phone number. I will carefully review your comments and share them with the author and editors who worked on the book.

Email: feedback@quepublishing.com

Mail: Greg Wiegand
            Associate Publisher
            Que Publishing
            800 East 96th Street
            Indianapolis, IN 46240 USA

Reader Services

Visit our website and register this book at informit.com/register for convenient access to any updates, downloads, or errata that might be available for this book.

In this chapter, you learn about the different BlackBerry Curve models, their external features, and the software you need to install on your PC or Mac. Topics include the following:

→ The three BlackBerry Curve models and their variants

→ External features

→ Device features

→ Required software and installation instructions

P

Prologue: Getting to Know the BlackBerry Curve Models

It is always good to start at the beginning when learning about a new device. Doing so allows you to learn about something from the ground up. If you have owned other BlackBerry models before, you may want to skip ahead to the chapters that will be most useful to you. If you have never used a BlackBerry, read on.

BlackBerry Curve 8300 Series

This was the very first BlackBerry Curve that Research In Motion (RIM) released, in June 2007. The BlackBerry Curve was a revolutionary BlackBerry, because prior to this original BlackBerry Curve 8300, full-keyboard BlackBerry models were very corporate, very purpose-built for the enterprise world of businesspeople. This BlackBerry added consumer features such as multi-media, 1/4" stereo headphone jack, expandable storage, and a camera.

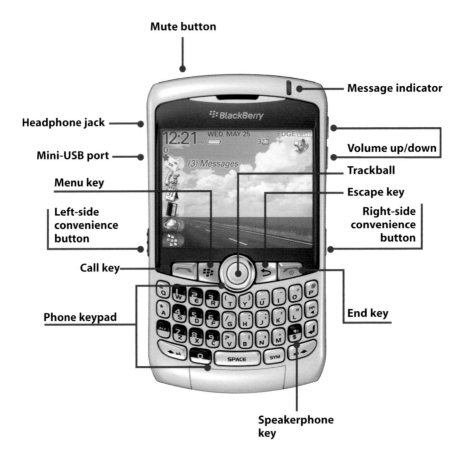

The original BlackBerry Curve was, and still is, very popular. RIM released variants of this model to address certain markets.

BlackBerry Curve 8310

The BlackBerry Curve 8310 is the same as the Curve 8300 in every way, except that it includes an onboard Global Positioning System (GPS) receiver.

BlackBerry Curve 8320

The BlackBerry Curve 8320 is the same as the Curve 8300 in every way, except that it includes an additional Wi-Fi radio onboard. This allows it to make use of Wi-Fi hot spots and the amazing cost-saving feature called Unlicensed Mobile Access (UMA).

BlackBerry Curve 8330

This BlackBerry Curve variant works on the Code Division Multiple Access (CDMA) and Evolution Data Only (EVDO) networks. The 8330 also includes a GPS receiver but no Wi-Fi radio.

BlackBerry Curve 8350i

In December 2008, the BlackBerry 8350i was released. This variant of the Curve is built for the Integrated Digital Enhanced Network (iDEN). This is typically used by blue-collar workers because it has a Push To Talk (PTT) feature that acts like a two-way radio or walkie-talkie. This last Curve 8300 variant also has a Wi-Fi radio and a GPS receiver.

To summarize, the original BlackBerry Curve 8300 has five variants:

- BlackBerry Curve 8300 (Original Curve, GSM/EDGE)
- BlackBerry Curve 8310 (GSM/EDGE, GPS receiver)

Push to talk button

- BlackBerry Curve 8320 (GSM/EDGE, Wi-Fi radio plus UMA)
- BlackBerry Curve 8330 (CDMA/EVDO, GPS receiver)
- BlackBerry Curve 8350i (iDEN, PTT, GPS receiver, Wi-Fi radio)

All the original BlackBerry Curve 8300 variants share the following characteristics:

- 320×240 pixel Quarter VGA (QVGA) screen
- 2-megapixel camera with a flash
- Same keyboard layout and size
- Trackball navigation

BlackBerry Curve 8900

The BlackBerry Curve 8900 built on the success of the Curve 8300 series and took the BlackBerry Curve brand to the next level. The BlackBerry Curve 8900 does not have variants—yet. The BlackBerry 8900 is a GSM device. No CDMA or other variants exist.

The BlackBerry Curve 8900 has the following characteristics:

- 480×360 pixel Half VGA (HVGA) screen
- 3.2-megapixel camera with a flash and autofocus
- Trackball navigation

BlackBerry Curve 8520

Rewind Play/pause   Fast-forward

Headphone jack

Micro-USB port

Volume up/down

Left-side convenience button

Right-side convenience button

Menu key

Escape key

Call key

End key

Phone keypad

Speakerphone key

Optical trackpad

The latest BlackBerry Curve is the Curve 8520, a mixture of the first two Curves with a twist. Even though the BlackBerry Curve 8520 is the newest Curve, it has the original Curve's 320×240 pixel screen and 2-megapixel camera.

The Curve 8520 does have some interesting features. It uses an optical track-pad instead of a trackball for navigation. This trackpad works like a touchpad on a laptop and reduces the moving parts of the BlackBerry Curve 8520 to zero. The Curve 8520 also has external dedicated multimedia buttons on the top for play/pause, fast-forward, and rewind.

The BlackBerry Curve 8520 has the following characteristics:

- 320×240 pixel Quarter VGA (QVGA) screen

- 2-megapixel camera without a flash

- Trackpad navigation

Note

Use the RIM-provided case or one you've purchased. It protects the vulnerable trackball, data port, and screen from damage.

All RIM devices have a one-year warranty to cover any manufacturing defects. A cracked screen, chipped case, nonfunctioning or missing trackball, damaged USB port, or drowned (water-damaged) BlackBerry are not covered by RIM's one-year warranty.

The BlackBerry Curve's External Features

The outside of any device is the part you will interact with the most, so let's start there.

BlackBerry Curve 8300 Series (8300, 8310, 8320, 8330, 8350i)

BlackBerry Curve 8300: Top

- Mute button

- Two speaker holes

Speaker holes

Mute button

BlackBerry Curve 8300: Left

- 3.5mm headphone jack (with the exception of the 8350i)
- Mini-USB port for charging and synchronizing
- Left-side convenience button (voice dialing)

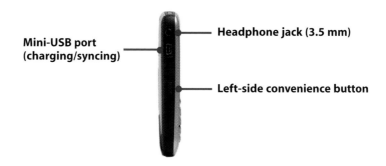

Mini-USB port (charging/syncing)

Headphone jack (3.5 mm)

Left-side convenience button

BlackBerry Curve 8300: Right

- Volume up/down buttons
- Right-side convenience button (camera)

Volume up/down buttons

Right-side convenience button

BlackBerry Curve 8300: Back

Flash

Camera

Self-portrait mirror

Battery door latch

Dock charging contact

- 2-megapixel camera with a flash
- Self-portrait mirror
- Battery door and latch

BlackBerry Curve 8300: Front

Light-emitting diode (LED)

Menu key

Trackball

Escape key

Call key

End key

Integrated phone keypad

Speakerphone key

Symbol key

- Light-emitting diode (LED)
- Trackball for navigation
- Call key
- End key
- Menu key
- Escape key
- QWERTY keyboard

BlackBerry Curve 8900

BlackBerry Curve 8900: Top

- Mute button
- Lock button
- Two speaker holes

BlackBerry Curve 8900: Left

Left-side convenience button

• Left-side convenience button (defaults to voice dialing)

BlackBerry Curve 8900: Right

Headphone jack

Volume up/down button

Right-side convenience button

Micro-USB port

- 3.5mm headphone jack
- Volume up/down button
- Right-side convenience button (camera)
- Micro-USB port for charging and synchronization

BlackBerry Curve 8900: Back

- 3.2-megapixel camera with a flash and autofocus
- Battery door and latch

BlackBerry Curve 8900: Front

- Light-emitting diode (LED)
- Trackball for navigation
- Call key
- End key

- Menu key
- Escape key
- QWERTY keyboard

BlackBerry Curve 8520

BlackBerry Curve 8520: Top

- Multimedia buttons (rewind, play/pause, fast-forward)
- Two speaker holes

BlackBerry Curve 8520: Left

Headphone jack ———

Micro-USB port

Left-side convenience button

- 3.5mm headphone jack
- Micro-USB port for charging and synchronizing
- Left-side convenience button (voice dialing)

BlackBerry Curve 8520: Right

Volume up/down buttons

Right-side convenience button

- Volume up/down button
- Right-side convenience button

BlackBerry Curve 8520: Back

Camera

Battery door latch

- 2-megapixel camera
- Battery door and latch

BlackBerry Curve 8520: Front

Optical trackpad

Light-emitting diode (LED)

Menu key

Call key

End key

Integrated phone keypad

Escape key

Alt key

Speakerphone key

Shift key

Symbol key

- Light-emitting diode (LED)
- Optical trackpad for navigation
- Call key
- End key
- Menu key
- Escape key
- QWERTY keyboard

Navigation and Typing

Navigating and typing are very important tasks, so let's briefly go over the basics.

Navigating

To navigate around screens and menus on your BlackBerry Curve, you must use the trackball, or the trackpad with the BlackBerry Curve 8520.

Lightly touch the trackball with your thumb. Move your thumb to roll the trackball in all directions to move around screens and menu options.

Press the trackball to make a selection on the screen. Pressing the trackball is the same as clicking a mouse on a computer.

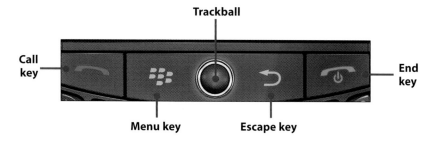

With the trackpad on the BlackBerry Curve 8520, lightly press your thumb on the trackpad and move it in all directions to move around screens and menus.

Press the trackpad to make a selection on the screen. Pressing the trackpad is the same as clicking a mouse on a computer.

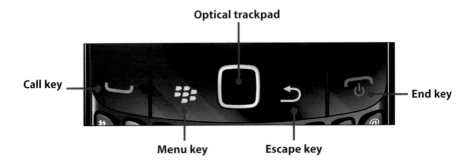

Optical trackpad

Call key

End key

Menu key   **Escape key**

If you are in a screen and you need to go back one step or screen, click the Escape key to the right of the trackball or trackpad.

To exit any program and return to the BlackBerry Home screen, click the End key.

The End button also doubles as the End Call key when you are on a call.

To bring up the phone application or to answer an incoming call, click the Call key.

When you want to bring up a menu on the BlackBerry Curve, press the trackball or trackpad. Think of this like clicking a mouse button. When you click the trackball or trackpad, a short menu appears on the screen. The short menus usually contain the choices you are looking for, so simply scroll up or down using the trackball or trackpad, and click to select the menu item.

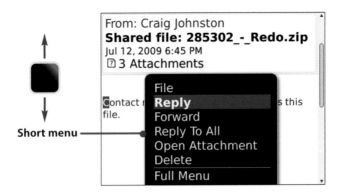

Short menu

If you want to bring up the full menu, click the Menu key, which is to the left of the trackball or trackpad. Again, scroll up or down the menu, and click to select your choice.

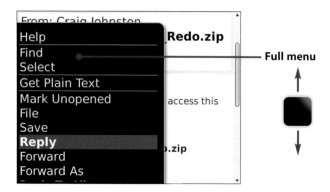

The BlackBerry Curve has two main screens. The first is called the Home Screen. It shows all your icons and folders. Folders are a way to group certain applications, such as Instant Messaging (IM) clients and games.

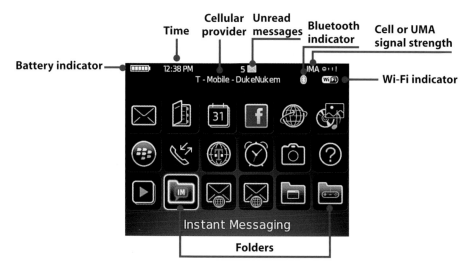

At the top of the screen, you can see a battery indicator; the time; indicators for unread messages, IM, or social networking (such as Facebook); a Bluetooth icon, a signal strength meter, and a Wi-Fi icon. You also see the cellular network you are connected to and the name of a Wi-Fi hot spot if you are connected to one.

The other main screen is called the Today screen. At the bottom of the Today screen, you see the top row of icons from the Home screen. Depending on the theme you use for your BlackBerry Curve (discussed in Chapter 11), these icons can also be along the left or right sides of the Today screen. At the top of the Today screen, you see the same indicators as on the Home screen.

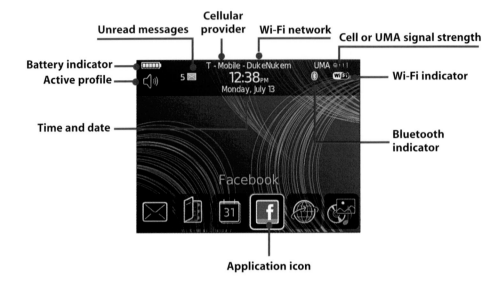

Typing

To type on your BlackBerry Curve, use the full keyboard under the screen. To type one of the alternative symbols on one of the keys, hold down the Alt key while pressing the desired key. For example, to type an exclamation point, hold down the Alt key and press the B key.

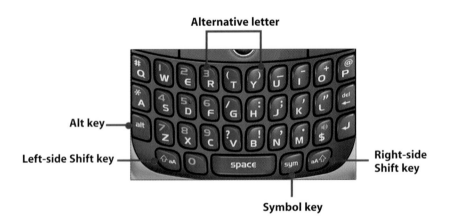

If you want to type a single capital letter, hold down the desired key for half a second. The letter changes to uppercase. To type a series of capital letters, engage the Caps Lock by holding down the Alt key and pressing the right-side Shift key. If you need to type a series of numbers or any series of alternative symbols, engage the Alt Lock by holding down the Alt key and pressing the left-side Shift key.

To select multiple lines of text, press and release the left-side Shift key, and use the trackball or trackpad to scroll up or down to select one or more lines of text.

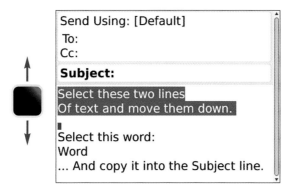

To select one or more letters, press and keep holding the left-side Shift key, and use the trackball or trackpad to scroll left or right to make the selection.

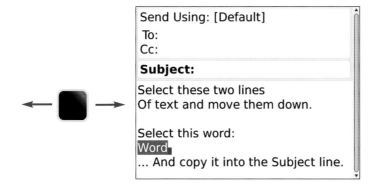

To copy your selection, press the Menu key and choose Copy.

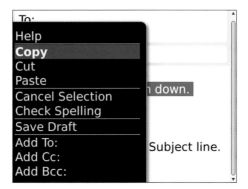

To paste the selected text, place the cursor where you want to paste the text, press the Menu key, and choose Paste.

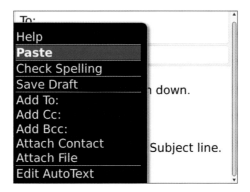

Installing the BlackBerry Desktop Software on Your Computer

The BlackBerry Curve is a smartphone that can operate without connecting to a computer. However, if you want to synchronize it with your calendar and address book, move multimedia onto your BlackBerry, perform a backup, or upgrade the device firmware, you need to install some software on your computer and connect your BlackBerry Curve using its USB cable.

Desktop Manager May Not Be Needed

If your BlackBerry Curve is on your company's BlackBerry Enterprise Server (BES), you probably won't need to install this software unless you want to move multimedia to and from your BlackBerry. This is because all synchronization is done wirelessly when you use a corporate BlackBerry.

Download the BlackBerry Desktop Software at http://na.blackberry.com/eng/services/desktop/. Select Download BlackBerry Desktop Software Including Service Packs. On the next screen, use the drop-down box to select BlackBerry Desktop Software 4.7, and click Next.

We May Be Behind the Times

Currently, 4.7 is the latest version. However, by the time you read this, a newer version may be available. It is a good rule of thumb to always download the latest version of the Desktop Software.

On the next screen, you see a list of a few versions of the software. You see these versions:

- Multilanguage without Media Manager
- Multilanguage with Media Manager
- English without Media Manager
- English with Media Manager

For the purposes of this book, it would be better if you selected the version that includes the Media Manager. We discuss the Media Manager in much more detail in Chapter 3, "Listening to Audio and Watching Video," so it would be easier if you installed it now.

When the file has been downloaded to your computer, double-click it to start the installation.

>>>*step-by-step*

Installing BlackBerry Desktop Manager on Microsoft Windows

1. On the first screen, click Next.

2. On the next screen, select your country or region, and click Next.

3. On the next screen, accept the agreement, and click Next.

4. On the next screen, click Next.

5. On the next screen, select the Typical installation, and click Next.

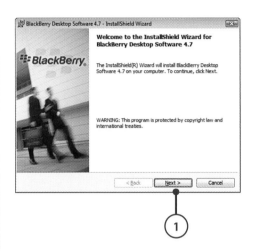

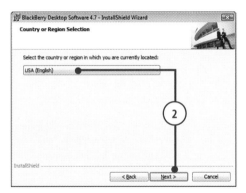

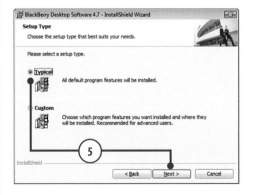

6. On the next screen, select Integrate with a personal email account, and click Next.

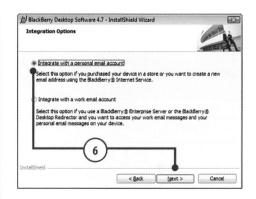

Desktop Manager in an Enterprise

You would select the other option only if you were using a corporate BlackBerry Curve and the BlackBerry administrator had specifically asked you to install the BlackBerry Desktop Software. Usually in a corporate environment, all synchronization and backup are done over the air, so there is no need for this software.

7. On the next screen, leave all options checked, and click Install.

8. When the installation is complete, you are asked to reboot your computer. Choose Yes, and allow your computer to reboot.

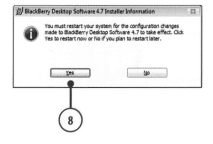

When your computer reboots, the BlackBerry Desktop Manager starts and asks you to connect your BlackBerry. For now, do not connect your BlackBerry, and click OK.

Installing PocketMac for BlackBerry and Missing Sync for BlackBerry on the Apple Macintosh OS X

If you use an Apple Macintosh running OS X, you have two options—Missing Sync for BlackBerry by Mark/Space, or PocketMac for BlackBerry.

Note

During post-production on this book, RIM released BlackBerry Desktop Manager for Mac. While it is too late to include it in this book, we will write a companion article on it at http://www.MyBlackBerryCurve.info.

BlackBerry Desktop Manager for Mac OS X is free and has the same functionality as the Windows version.

This book covers both PocketMac for BlackBerry and Missing Sync for BlackBerry, but we encourage you to choose only one of these applications, because you cannot install both of them on your Mac; you must pick one or the other. PocketMac for BlackBerry is available for free from the BlackBerry website, whereas Missing Sync costs $39.95.

>>>*step-by-step*

PocketMac for BlackBerry

1. Download PocketMac for BlackBerry and Driver Update for PocketMac at http://na. blackberry.com/eng/services/ desktop/mac.jsp.

2. After both files have been down-loaded, you see both icons on your desktop. Double-click the icon labeled PocketMac for BlackBerry. The PocketMac for BlackBerry installer opens. Double-click the icon labeled PocketMac for BlackBerry 4.1.

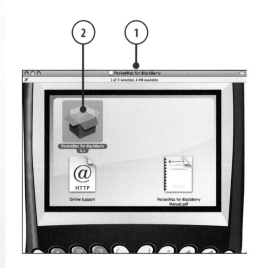

3. The PocketMac installer prompts you to enter your password to continue the installation. Type your Mac account password, and click OK.

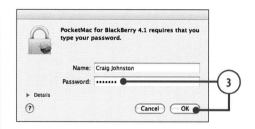

4. Click Next on the Release Notes and License Agreement screens. Then, on the Installation Type screen, click Install.

5. The next screen warns that no applications can be running during the installation. Click the Continue button. All the applications are closed, and the installation continues.

6. When the installation is complete, you see a message asking you to reboot your Mac to complete the installation. Click the Restart button, and your Mac restarts.

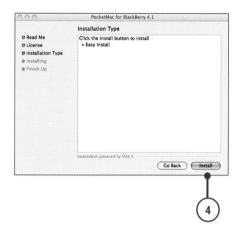

7. After your Mac reboots, you need to install the Driver Update. Because you rebooted, the Driver Update icon is no longer visible on your Desktop. You can find it in the Downloads folder under your user folder. Double-click the icon labeled DriverUpdate*XXX*.dmg, where *XXX* represents the version of the driver update.

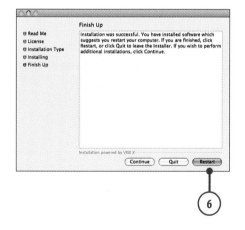

8. The Driver Update installer opens. Double-click the icon to begin the installation.

9. On the Select Destination screen, select your Macintosh's hard drive. This is usually called Macintosh HD. Click the Continue button.

10. When the installation is complete, again you are asked to restart your Mac. Click the Restart button.

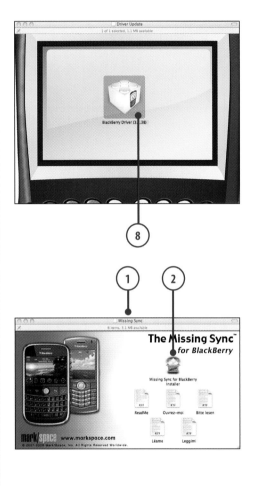

>>>step-by-step

Missing Sync for BlackBerry

1. Download Missing Sync for BlackBerry at http://www.markspace.com/products/blackberry/blackberry-sync-mac-software.html.

2. Double-click the file to start the installation. The Missing Sync for BlackBerry Main Installer screen appears. Double-click the icon labeled Missing Sync for BlackBerry Installer.

3. Unlike PocketMac for BlackBerry, Missing Sync for BlackBerry requires a piece of software to be installed on your BlackBerry Curve to synchronize it with your Mac. The installer's Introduction screen reminds you of this and tells you where to download it directly to your BlackBerry.

How to Install the BlackBerry Part of Missing Sync

Use your BlackBerry's browser to go to http://mirror.markspace.com/bb2.jad to install Missing Sync for BlackBerry on your Curve.

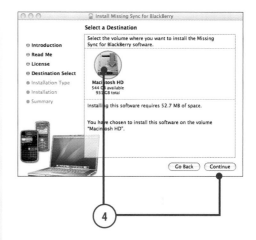

4. When you get to the Destination screen, click the hard drive where you want to install Missing Sync for BlackBerry. This is usually the hard drive called Macintosh HD. After you make the selection, click Continue.

5. Click Continue on the next few screens, and allow Missing Sync for BlackBerry to be installed. You need to reboot your Mac at the end of the installation.

Using This Book

My BlackBerry Curve was written to help you become very familiar with your BlackBerry Curve so that you can use it as efficiently as possible, get more done with it, and personalize it. If you have already flipped through the book, you have noticed that everything is explained through the help of full-color screenshots of a BlackBerry Curve. Many step-by-step instructions help guide you through each process.

Your BlackBerry Curve can synchronize with Microsoft Windows and Apple Mac OS X, so we cover both platforms. All procedures involving synchronizing with a computer are covered in Windows and OS X.

Although all the screenshots in this book were taken from a BlackBerry Curve 8900, anytime there are slight differences in the procedure, we mention it so that you won't get lost. Because the BlackBerry Curve is so customizable using themes, you may sometimes find that we mention an icon or folder on the BlackBerry Home screen that you may not see. This is normally because that icon has been moved to a folder by the theme you are using. The folder normally is named appropriately, so you should be able to find it easily.

It's Not All Good

Your BlackBerry Curve is an amazing smartphone that can do many things very well. However, it is not perfect, and we will point out those imperfections in the It's Not All Good sidebars.

>>> Go Further

Because there is limited space in this book, if there is something that we think may be useful for you to explore further, we mention it in these sidebars.

Type of network

Signal strength

Profile (ring tone)

Call key

Phone keypad

End key

Speakerphone key

In this chapter, you learn how to use your BlackBerry Curve to make, receive, and manage calls. You also learn how to customize your BlackBerry Curve's phone application and work with ring tones. Topics include the following:

1

→ Creating and using ring tones
→ Working with profiles
→ Unlicensed Mobile Access (UMA)
→ Phone options and settings

Making, Receiving, and Managing Calls

The BlackBerry Curve is a great smartphone that has a lot of features, but it's still a phone. The BlackBerry Curve's phone integrates neatly into the BlackBerry software, which allows it to have some extra features not found on regular cell phones.

Configuring Phone Settings

Let's start with the phone configuration. You can completely customize how the phone works and sounds and make it uniquely yours. You might not want your BlackBerry Curve to sound like everyone else's phone—you can change the ring tone and set special ring tones to play when certain people call you.

In addition to ring tones, you can change some phone settings so that your ID is hidden when you call someone, or call waiting is disabled.

Creating Your Own Ring Tones

The ultimate way to personalize your BlackBerry Curve is to get a unique ring tone. Before we get into how to set up ring tones and other features, let's discuss how to create a custom ring tone and get it onto your BlackBerry.

The BlackBerry Curve can use many different file formats as a ring tone. The following formats are supported:

- 3gp
- WAV
- MIDI
- AMR-NB
- G711u/A, GSM610
- PCM
- MP3
- AAC/AAC+/eAAC+
- WMA9/10 Standard/Pro

As you can see, you have many choices when it comes to the ring tone formats. But how can you create your own ring tones? The easiest way is to use a website that allows you to upload an MP3, select the part of the song you want as your ring tone, and send that to your BlackBerry Curve.

>>>step-by-step

Creating Ring Tones with Mobicious

Many sites do this very well. Some charge, others are free, and still others are partially free. A great site that allows you to do all this for free is Mobicious. Here is how to use Mobicious:

1. Visit the Mobicious website on your desktop at http://www.mobicious.com/.

2. Sign up for a free account.

3. Click Make My Ringtone.

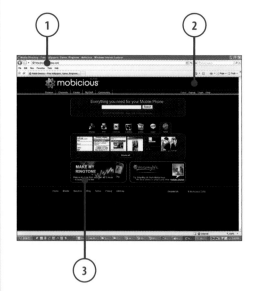

4. On the Create a Ringtone screen, click the Choose File button to select an MP3 file on your computer.

5. After choosing the file, click the Upload MP3 button.

6. On the Edit Ringtone screen, drag the blue bar to the part of the song you want to use for your ring tone.

7. Click the Send to My Mobile Phone button.

8. Type your phone number.

9. Select your wireless carrier.

10. Click the Send to Phone button.

11. You receive an SMS or text message on your BlackBerry. Open the SMS, click the link, and choose Save.

12. Backspace over the filename, and change it from the number to something more recognizable, like the song's name.

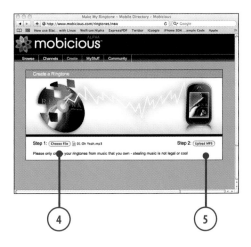

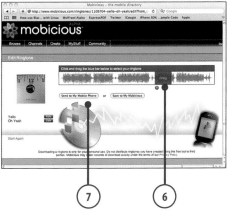

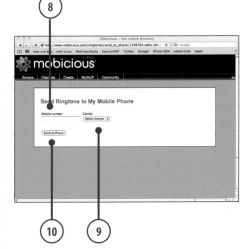

Setting Phone Sounds

Whether or not you create your own ring tones, you may want to personalize how your BlackBerry Curve's phone sounds. All sound settings for the BlackBerry Curve are set in the Profiles application, which you can find on the Home Screen.

1. Open the Profiles application.

2. To edit a profile, scroll to Advanced, and click the trackball or trackpad.

3. Scroll to the profile you want to edit, click the Menu button, and choose Edit.

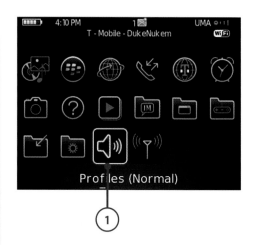

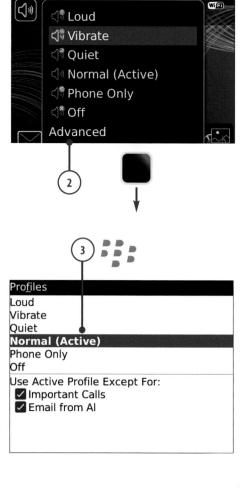

4. This list is expanded when you install new applications that have their own new sounds. For example, if you install AOL Instant Messenger (AIM), you see a couple new sounds called AIM Alert and AIM New Message. Take some time and scroll through all the available sounds or alerts on this screen.

5. To edit the Phone sounds, scroll down to Phone, and click the trackball or trackpad.

The top half shows the alerts that play when your BlackBerry Curve is out of its holster. The bottom half shows the alerts that play when your BlackBerry is in its holster.

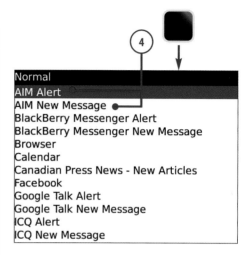

Normal
AIM Alert
AIM New Message
BlackBerry Messenger Alert
BlackBerry Messenger New Message
Browser
Calendar
Canadian Press News - New Articles
Facebook
Google Talk Alert
Google Talk New Message
ICQ Alert
ICQ New Message

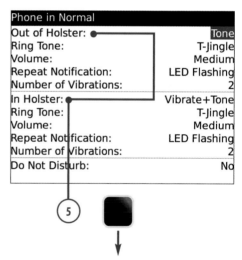

Phone in Normal
Out of Holster: Tone
Ring Tone: T-Jingle
Volume: Medium
Repeat Notification: LED Flashing
Number of Vibrations: 2
In Holster: Vibrate+Tone
Ring Tone: T-Jingle
Volume: Medium
Repeat Notification: LED Flashing
Number of Vibrations: 2
Do Not Disturb: No

We should probably take a moment to explain this concept, because it is unique to the BlackBerry. In 1999, when the BlackBerry was a hard-core business tool, it was sold with a holster. The holster clipped onto your belt and allowed you to quickly grab your BlackBerry, read email, reply to email, and return it to its holster. In those days one-way pagers were popular, and they had holsters, so it seemed a natural progression to sell the BlackBerry with a holster.

RIM decided that the BlackBerry should be aware of its location, either in the holster or out of the holster. This made sense, because you might want to set your BlackBerry to vibrate or play a sound when it is in its holster on your belt. But when you take it out of its holster to reply to emails, it doesn't need to vibrate or play a sound, because you have it in your hand, and can see the new email arrive.

The second reason for this awareness is that when your BlackBerry is in its holster, it puts itself into sleep mode, where it turns off the screen and disables the keyboard. This saves battery life and prevents accidental key pressing (also called pocket dialing).

Every BlackBerry since the inception of the BlackBerry has been aware of its location, either in the holster or out of the holster. It knows if it is in the holster or out of the holster because it has a little micro switch that is triggered by a small magnet in the holster. When you clip your BlackBerry into its holster, the magnet activates the micro switch.

Since then, the BlackBerry has become trendy and has been adopted by the consumer marketplace. The BlackBerry is no longer sold with a traditional holster, but with a case. Sometimes the BlackBerry is sold without any kind of holster or case, which means you need to buy your own.

It's Not All Good

When buying a case or holster for your BlackBerry Curve, you should know what to look for. Some case manufacturers do not follow the design specifications for BlackBerry cases and holsters, and they do not include the small magnet. Without the magnet, your BlackBerry doesn't know when it is in its holster. If it doesn't know this, it cannot go to sleep or disable the keyboard. Not disabling the keyboard means that it could accidentally dial someone. Not going to sleep means that the battery will not last as long. This ultimately means that you cannot take full advantage of the profiles.

The top half of the Out of Holster/In Holster screen has the following options:
- Out of Holster:
    - None
    - Tone
    - Vibrate
    - Vibrate + Tone

- Ring Tone:
    - Click the trackball or trackpad to see a list of ring tones.
    - Scroll to the top of the list to see the custom ring tones you may have downloaded.
- Volume:
    - Mute
    - Low
    - Medium
    - High
    - Escalating (starts soft and gets progressively louder)
- Repeat Notification:
    - None
    - LED Flashing (an LED flashes after a missed call for visual notification)
- Number of Vibrations (used only if Out of Holster is set to Vibrate or Vibrate and Tone):
    - 1
    - 2
    - 3

The bottom half of the screen has the same settings as the top half, but these are the settings for when your BlackBerry is in its holster.

The final line on this screen is Do Not Disturb. If you change this to Yes, your BlackBerry does not alert you in any way when a call comes in. Instead, it sends the call straight to voice mail. This setting is unique to the Phone part of a BlackBerry profile.

To save your settings, click the Escape button and choose Save.

Specifying a Ring Tone by Creating an Exception

In addition to regular profiles, you can override the sound that is played based on who is calling you. This allows you to set up a special ring tone for a group of people or just one person. To do this, follow these steps:

1. Go back to the main Profiles screen, click the Menu button, and choose New Exception.

2. On the next screen, type the name of the exception in the Exception field.

3. On the next line, click the track-ball or trackpad, and choose Add Name. This brings up the Contacts.

4. Choose a name from your Contacts. You can repeat steps 3 and 4 to add more names to this field.

5. Leave the next line set to Active Profile.

6. On the last line, click to see a list of ring tones, and choose one.

7. Press the Escape button to save your settings.

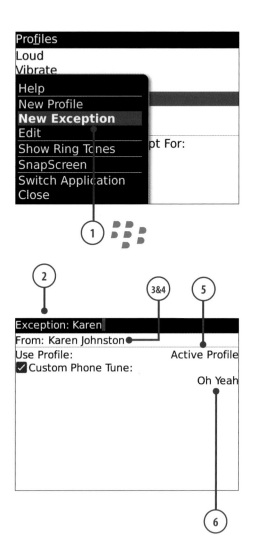

Note

By leaving this line set to Active Profile, you are telling your BlackBerry to always apply this exception, no matter which profile is selected. If you change it to a specific profile name, this tells your BlackBerry to apply this exception only when that particular profile is selected. For example, if you set this field to Quiet, this tells your BlackBerry to apply this exception only when you have your BlackBerry set to Quiet. If your BlackBerry is set to Normal or Loud or any other profile, this exception is ignored.

Specifying a Ring Tone Without Creating an Exception

Last, you can specify a ring tone for any of your contacts without having to create exceptions.

Unlike an exception, this ring tone plays only if the profile you have selected is set to play a sound. In other words, selecting a custom ring tone for a particular contact simply overrides the tune selected in the active profile. If that active profile is set not to play a sound, no sound is played. This is unlike an exception that is truly an exception to the rule, which plays the ring tone in that exception even if the active profile is quiet.

>>>*step-by-step*

1. From the BlackBerry Home Screen, click Contacts.

2. Scroll to the contact you want to add a custom ring tone for.

3. Click the Menu button, and choose Edit.

4. Click the trackball or trackpad, and choose Add Custom Ring Tone.

5. A new field called Custom Ring Tone appears at the bottom of the contact.

6. Click Browse to choose from the available ring tones.

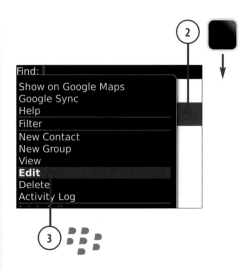

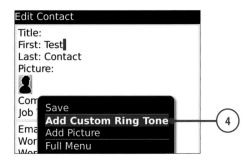

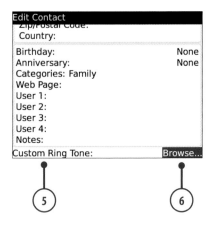

7. Press the Escape button and choose Save when you are finished.

Choose a ring tone

>>>step-by-step

Setting Phone Sounds

Besides the BlackBerry profile settings that control how the phone sounds, you can change other phone settings to further customize your phone experience.

1. Press the Call button to jump to the Phone application.

2. Click the Menu button, and choose Options.

3. On the Phone Options screen, click General Options.

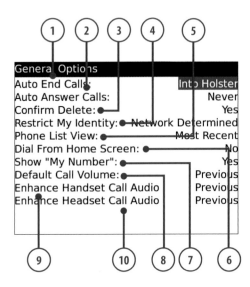

General Options

1. Auto End Calls can be set to Never and Into Holster. If you change it to Into Holster, your BlackBerry ends the active phone call when you put it in a holster or case. Remember that the holster or case you are using must have the small magnet that allows your BlackBerry to be aware.

2. Auto Answer Calls can be set to Never and Out of Holster. If you set it to Out of Holster, your BlackBerry automatically answers all incoming phone calls when it detects that it is out of its holster or case.

3. Next is Confirm Delete. By default, when you click a number in the phone list and choose Delete, you are prompted to confirm that you want to delete the number. If you set this to No, you are not prompted.

4. Restrict My Identity can be set to Always, Never, and Network Determined. If you set it to Always, your BlackBerry does not send your Caller ID information. If you set it to Never, your BlackBerry always sends your Caller ID information. If you set it to Network Determined, your BlackBerry does not try to override whatever your carrier has set your Caller ID restrictions to.

5. Phone List View controls what you see when you open the phone application. The choices are Most Recent, Most Used, Name, and Call Log. Most Recent displays the most recently called numbers. Most Used displays the most-called numbers. Name sorts the list of numbers by the names in your Address Book if you have them. Call Log shows a log of the numbers you've dialed.

6. Dial From Home Screen allows you to be able to pick up your BlackBerry Curve and, without first switching to the Phone application, start dialing numbers right on the keypad. If you set this feature to No, you can't dial directly from your BlackBerry Curve's Home Screen. First you must enter the phone application by pressing the green Call button.

Dial From Home Screen

The benefit of setting this feature to No is that it allows you to use application shortcuts from the Home Screen that let you press a single letter to launch different BlackBerry applications. We will discuss this in more detail later.

7. Next is Show "My Number." If you set this to No, the phone application does not display your phone number on the main phone screen. However, it still shows your number while you're on a phone call.

8. Default Call Volume defaults to Previous, which means that the call volume of your next phone call will be the same as your previous call. This setting can be set to 25%, 50%, 75%, or 100%. If you specify a value, each new phone call has the volume set to that particular value.

9. Enhance Handset Call Audio defaults to Previous, which means that any audio enhancement you selected during your last call also is set on any new phone calls. The settings can be Normal, which means no enhancement; Boost Bass, which boosts the bass of the incoming audio; and Boost Treble, which boosts the treble of the incoming audio.

10. The final setting on this screen is Enhanced Headset Call Audio. This is identical to the previous setting but relates to a headset. The headset could be a Bluetooth headset or a regular cable-connected headset.

11. When you have changed your settings, press the Escape button to go back one screen.

>>>*step-by-step*

Voice Mail

1. Click Voice Mail.

2. The Voice Mail screen has only two fields. These fields normally are preset by your carrier, so you should not need to change them. However, if you decide to use a voice mail system that is not provided by your carrier, you can use this screen to set the voice mail access number and a password if needed.

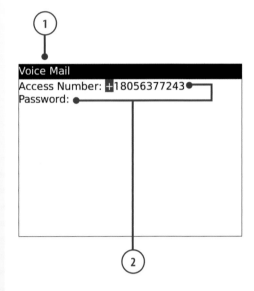

Why Change Voice Mail Number

Typical uses of a noncarrier voice mail system is when you want to use a voice mail system that translates the voice mail audio into text and then emails the text of that voice mail to your BlackBerry. However, there could be many reasons why you want to use an alternative voice mailbox, such as Google Voice.

3. When you have changed your settings, press the Escape button to go back one screen.

Call Logging

1. Click Call Logging.

2. This allows you to set what your BlackBerry logs when you receive calls. You can set it to Missed Calls, All Calls, or None. If you set this to Missed Calls or All Calls, the call information appears in your BlackBerry Messages view among your emails.

3. When you have changed your settings, press the Escape button to go back one screen.

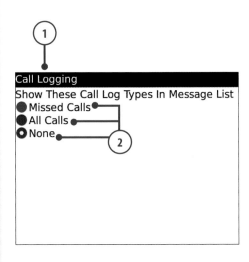

Call Forwarding

Note

When you select Call Forwarding, your BlackBerry first queries the carrier network to find out how you have your call forwarding set up. This means that you need to be in wireless coverage to change these settings.

Normally your call forwarding is set to forward calls to your voice mailbox if you do not answer them. However, you can reconfigure the settings so that calls are forwarded to another phone number.

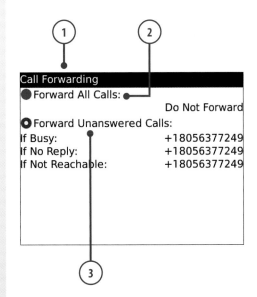

1. Click Call Forwarding.

2. The first setting is Forward All Calls. This is normally set to Do Not Forward. If you scroll to the setting Do Not Forward and click the trackball or trackpad, you can choose a number to forward all calls to. By default this is set to your voice mailbox number. However, if you want to add numbers to the list of choices, first click the Menu button and choose New Number. This brings up a screen that allows you to enter more phone numbers as possible forwarding numbers. After you have done this, when you click Do Not Forward, you can select from a list of numbers instead of just your voice mailbox number.

    If you choose to forward all calls to a specific number, your BlackBerry ignores the other settings on this screen.

3. The other settings are under Forward Unanswered Calls. These are If Busy, If No Reply, and If Not Reachable. Again, to change the number that the calls are forwarded to, click the number next to the setting, and you can select a new number from the list.

4. When you have changed your settings, press the Escape button to go back one screen.

>>>step-by-step

Call Waiting

1. Click Call Waiting.

2. The only choices here are Yes and No. Set this to No to disable the Call Waiting feature on your BlackBerry. When this is disabled, you are not audibly notified when you receive a call while on another call.

3. When you have changed your settings, press the Escape button to go back one screen.

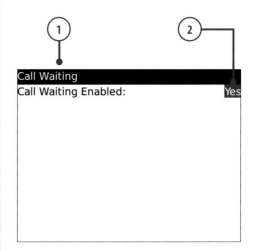

Note
When you select Call Waiting, your BlackBerry first queries the carrier network to find out how you have your call forwarding set up. This means that you need to be in wireless coverage to change these settings.

Smart Dialing

1. Click Smart Dialing.

    This screen allows your BlackBerry to handle phone numbers more intelligently and allows you to configure your BlackBerry to dial internal company numbers.

2. First you need to set the Country Code. This is the code that people use when they need to call your country. For example, the United States is 1, the United Kingdom is 44, and South Africa is 27. You always put a plus sign ahead of the number. So the United States would be +1, and the United Kingdom would be +44, for example.

3. The Area Code field you can leave blank, but if you call a certain area code frequently, enter it here.

4. National Number Length is the length of phone numbers in your country. To calculate the number length, count the number of digits in your phone number without any country codes or dialing area codes. For example, if your full number is +1 212 555-1212, the +1 is the country code, so the remaining number of digits is 10.

5. If you use your BlackBerry for business and you normally use it to call colleagues, it may be useful to fill in the fields in the next section. Enter your company's phone number in the field To access office extensions within my corporation, call Number. Next, choose how many seconds your BlackBerry must wait before dialing the extension. The default is 3 seconds. Finally, you can specify the extension length.

6. The last section is for dialing numbers in other corporations. Here you can set how many seconds your BlackBerry must wait before dialing the extension. This last section works in conjunction with another BlackBerry phone feature. That is the BlackBerry's ability to dial extensions.

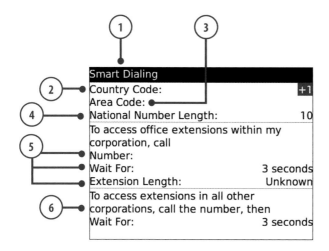

To take advantage of this feature, when you enter your contact's office phone numbers into your Contacts, enter the company's number, and then type an X and the person's extension. For example, you would enter +1 212 555-1212 X 1234. In the future, if you choose to dial this person from your Contacts, your BlackBerry would dial +1 212 555-1212, wait for the time you specify on this screen (a default of 3 seconds), and then dial the numbers following the X.

Note

Normally when you dial phone numbers within a country, you add a number before the area code. For example, in South Africa, to dial Durban on area code 31, you dial 031. The 0 is an instruction number. When calculating your National Number Length, you do not include this instruction number.

---

7. When you have changed your settings, press the Escape button to go back one screen.

>>>*step-by-step*

Speed Dial Numbers

This screen allows you to set up phone numbers associated with letters on the keyboard.

1. Click Speed Dial Numbers.

2. To set a letter to a speed dial, scroll to the letter, click the trackball or trackpad, and choose New Speed Dial. This opens your BlackBerry Contacts and allows you to choose the person to assign to that particular letter.

3. When you have changed your settings, press the Escape button to go back one screen.

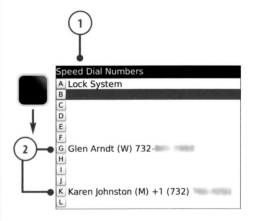

Note

To use speed-dial numbers, you first assign each number to a letter on this screen. Then, on the Home Screen, you press and hold the appropriate key, and your BlackBerry dials that number.

By default, the letter A is set to lock your BlackBerry, Q is set to Change Profile to Vibrate, and W is set to Voice Mail, and they cannot be changed. You can use all other letters for your speed-dial numbers.

 >>>step-by-step

FDN Phone List

1. Click FDN Phone List.

2. When you have changed your settings, press the Escape button to go back one screen.

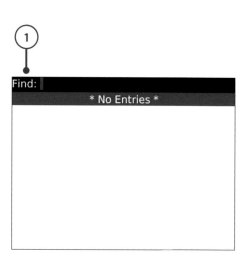

Find:

* No Entries *

Note

FDN stands for Fixed Dialing Numbers. When you enable this feature, your BlackBerry can dial only the numbers you type in this list.

To enable the FDN Phone List, you must choose a personal identification number (PIN). This PIN is required if you want to enable, disable, or change the FDN Phone List.

The typical purpose of this feature would be if you lend your BlackBerry Curve to someone and you want to limit who the person can call. Another purpose would be a parent using this feature to limit who his or her child calls.

Making Calls

Now that you know how to fully customize your BlackBerry Curve's phone experience, you are ready to make some phone calls.

Dialing with the Keypad

Every BlackBerry Curve has a phone keypad right on the keyboard. It is laid out in a very similar way to a regular cell phone or home phone keypad. On a BlackBerry Curve with a QWERTY keyboard, the W, E, R, S, D, F, Z, X, and C keys double as the 1, 2, 3, 4, 5, 6, 7, 8, and 9, respectively. The 0 key is on its own, to the left of the spacebar. Unlike a regular phone keypad, the Q key doubles as the # key, and the A key doubles as the * key.

One extra key on the keyboard that is important is the $ key. This key doubles as the speakerphone key; you see a little speaker symbol on it. When you are on a call, pressing this key activates the speakerphone, allowing you to put your BlackBerry Curve on a solid surface and use it as a speakerphone.

There are two places where you can use the keypad for dialing:

- One is on the Home Screen. If you start typing the phone number on the phone keypad, your BlackBerry Curve automatically jumps into the phone application. You do not need to hold down the Alt key while typing the numbers, because your BlackBerry Curve expects you to type phone numbers.

- The other place where you can use the keypad is the phone application itself. When you press the green Call button, start dialing the phone number using the keypad. Again, you do not need to hold down the Alt key to get to the numbers. Your BlackBerry Curve knows that you do not want to type the letters.

You are probably wondering how you would dial phone numbers made up of letters, such as 1 800 MYCURVE. As you know, ever since anyone can remember, the phone keypad has included letters on its keys. For example, the 2 key has ABC, the 3 key has DEF, and so on. On a regular phone keypad, you would simply press the key that corresponds to a letter in the phone number. For example, if you dialed 1 800 MYCURVE on a regular phone keypad, you would get 1 800 692-8783.

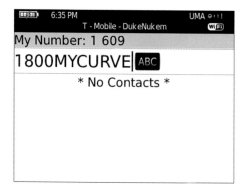

To do this using the BlackBerry Curve keyboard, start dialing the number. When you come to the letters, hold down the Alt key and type the part of the phone number that contains letters using the regular keyboard. So you would type 1800, press and hold the Alt key, and then type MYCURVE. On the phone application screen, you see 1800MYCURVE, but when you press the Call button to dial, you see the actual numbers being dialed, 1 800 692-8783.

Other Ways of Dialing with the Phone Application

While we still have the Phone application open, let's explore other ways to dial numbers from within it. You may have already noticed that there is a list of phone numbers. This is your phone list.

Click to call —

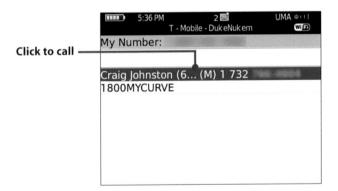

If you scroll down the list to one of the numbers, you can click the trackball or trackpad, and the menu pops up with the choice call selected. To dial it, just click again.

>>>step-by-step

Dialing Using Contacts

Another way that you can dial numbers on the BlackBerry Curve is to use your Contacts.

1. From the Home Screen, use the trackball or trackpad to move the cursor over the Contacts icon, and click.

2. When the Contacts application opens, you can find who you need to call by typing his or her name. As you type, your BlackBerry Curve automatically filters the list of contacts until you find the person you are looking for.

3. After you have found the person, scroll to his or her name and click the trackball or trackpad. This shows you the contact information for this person.

Note

If you have entered multiple numbers for the one contact, all numbers are displayed, such as Work, Home, and Mobile.

4. Scroll to the number you want to use, and click the trackball or trackpad again. This brings up a menu that shows "Call" and the number you selected. For example, if you click the Mobile number, it shows "Call Mobile." To call that number, simply click again, and the phone calls that person's mobile number.

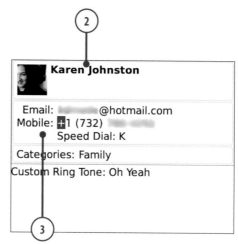

A Faster Way to Dial

A quicker way to dial a particular contact is to not click into the person's information first. Instead, scroll down to the contact in the list, and click the Menu button. Scroll down to Call, and click the trackball or trackpad. If multiple numbers are entered for this contact, they are listed on the screen for you to choose from.

Dialing from an Email or Web Page

The BlackBerry Curve is always on the lookout for phone numbers. Whenever you are reading emails or browsing the Internet, if your BlackBerry sees a phone number, it underlines it and makes it clickable.

Click to dial

Note

The BlackBerry Curve uses some built-in logic to figure out if a number it sees is a phone number, but you can make this function more accurate by making sure that you fill in the Smart Dialing section in the Phone Options that we discussed earlier. The most important field to fill in is the National Number Length.

As you read through emails or view web pages, scroll to a phone number, click the trackball or trackpad, and choose "Call <number>." The menu item displays the number from the web page or email. Click again to dial.

Dialing Using Your Voice

The BlackBerry Curve has a voice dialing feature. This is useful because it enables you to dial numbers in your address book by speaking the contact's name. Besides being convenient, it is safe to use while driving because you can call without taking your eyes off the road.

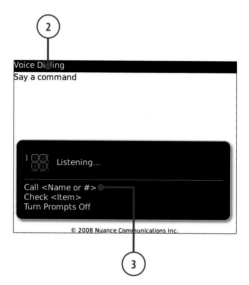

Voice Dialing
Say a command

Listening...

Call <Name or #>
Check <Item>
Turn Prompts Off

© 2008 Nuance Communications Inc.

1. To activate this feature, simply press and release the left-side convenience button.

2. Your BlackBerry verbally instructs you to "Say a command" and plays a sound.

3. Say "Call" and the name of the person you want to call from your Contacts, such as "Call Craig Johnston." Your BlackBerry repeats your command and starts dialing the number.

   If the person you are calling has more than one number, you can indicate which number you want to call. For example, you could say "Call Craig Johnston home" to call Craig Johnston at his home number.

   If you forget to say which number to use, your BlackBerry asks you before it dials. You can just say "home" or "mobile" or whichever number you want to call. Your BlackBerry then dials that number.

Dialing While Driving

Dialing with your voice is the safest way to make calls while you are driving, because it allows you to keep your mind on the road.

You can also use numbers when calling via voice dialing.

1. Press the Voice Dialing button, wait for the prompt "Say a command," and say "Call 2125551212" to call 212 555-1212.

2. Your BlackBerry repeats the numbers you told it to call and asks you if this is correct. Then it plays a sound.

3. After the sound, say "Yes" if the number is correct, and your BlackBerry dials it.

Voice Dialing and Headsets

You can use voice dialing while using a headset. If you are using a headset connected to your BlackBerry Curve via a cable, press and hold the call answer/hang-up button until you hear voice dialing prompt you with "Say a command," and then proceed as before.

If you are using a Bluetooth headset, press and release the call answer/hang-up button, wait for your BlackBerry to prompt you with "Say a command," and then proceed as before.

Volume up/down buttons

Managing In-Progress Calls

While you are on a phone call, you can do a number of things.

To adjust the volume, use the volume up/down buttons on the top right of your BlackBerry.

To place a call on hold, click the Menu button and choose Hold. When a call is on hold, you can initiate a new call, complete that new call, and return to the call you placed on hold.

Speakerphone button

Select to place a call on hold

Select to Add Participant to a three-way call

Select to enhance audio

Select to move between your headset and speakerphone

You can add a participant to the current call. This feature works only if your wireless carrier supports three-way calling and you subscribe to this feature. Click the Menu button and choose Add Participant. Your BlackBerry shows you your phone list and also allows you to browse your Contacts if the person you need to call is not in your phone list.

To move the call from your BlackBerry to your Bluetooth headset, click the trackball or trackpad, and choose Activate Headset. This transfers the call from your BlackBerry to your headset.

To enhance the call audio during a call, click the trackball or trackpad, and choose Enhance Call Audio. Your choices for enhancement are Boost Bass and Boost Treble.

After you make your selection, an icon appears on the phone screen, indicating that you are using enhanced audio.

Note

This feature does not work when you are using the speakerphone.

If you want to take a few notes while on a call, click the Menu button, and choose Notes. These notes will be attached to that particular phone call in the call log, allowing you to go back and read the notes associated with that call.

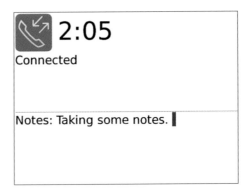

Because the notes you take are saved in the call log for that particular phone call, the only way to view and forward the notes is to change your Phone List View to Call Log under the General Phone Options we discussed earlier.

When you are displaying the Call Log, scroll to the call, press the Menu button, and click View History. This shows you a view that lists all the calls to and from that particular phone number, and when they occurred. As you scroll through the call times, the Duration field changes to display the duration of each call.

If you click the Menu button while a call is selected, you can forward the call log information for that particular call to someone via email. To do this, select Forward. Your BlackBerry composes a new email automatically for you and includes all the information about that call and any notes you took during the call.

If you want to add notes about the call after the fact, scroll down to that call in the list, click the Menu button, and choose Add Notes. If that call already has notes, you see Edit Notes. Select Edit Notes to edit or add to the notes previously taken for that call.

To look up something or work on something on your BlackBerry Curve while on a call, click the Menu button. Your choices are View Contacts, View Calendar, View Messages, and Switch Application.

If you choose Switch Application, your BlackBerry displays a list of applications that are already running and allows you to choose which one to switch to.

Applications to choose —

Note
No matter which choice you make, the call you are on is not dropped. This allows you to return to it after you exit the application you chose to switch to.

Receiving Calls

Answering calls on your BlackBerry Curve is not complicated, but it is good to know some of your options.

Answering Calls

No matter what you are doing on your BlackBerry, when someone calls you, you are interrupted with a screen of two choices—Answer and Ignore. The Answer choice is above the Call button, and Ignore is above the End button. If you choose to ignore the call, it goes to voice mail.

Answering Call Waiting Calls

If someone calls you while you are on another call, your BlackBerry Curve gives you a few choices. It adjusts the bottom of the display to show three options—Answer, More, and Ignore. Answer lets you answer the incoming call. Ignore sends the incoming call to voice mail. More gives you more options.

When you click the trackball or trackpad, a menu is displayed with a few more options. One is Answer - Hold Current, which answers the incoming call and puts the current call on hold. The second option is Answer - Drop Current, which answers the incoming call and drops the current call.

Managing Calls

Making and receiving calls in real time is one thing, but what if you need to work with missed calls or add notes to a call for your records? We will show you how to do that and more.

>>>step-by-step

Working with Missed Calls

If you do not answer an incoming call right away, it is listed in your call log and phone list in the Phone application. You also see an indication that you missed a call, or several calls, when a phone icon appears at the top of your BlackBerry screen with a number next to it.

To see the missed calls, click the Call button to jump into the Phone application.

1. If you want to make it a little easier to see your missed calls and take action on them, you can set the Phone application to Call Logging in the Phone Options.

2. In the Phone application, click the Menu button, and choose Options.

3. Scroll down to the Call Logging, and click.

4. If you change the setting to Missed Calls, this makes the BlackBerry list the missed calls in the Messages application.

5. This means that anytime you miss a call, the information about that call appears in the Messages application, along with your regular emails.

Taking Notes

If you use your BlackBerry for work, logging in the Messages application and taking notes on calls can be very useful. This is especially true when you're required to bill for time. You can keep a record of who called, when they called, and how long you spoke. You also can use your notes for later reference.

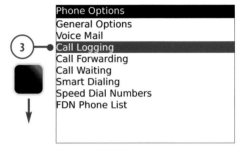

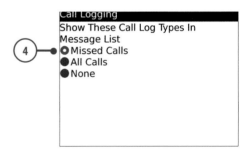

6. If you click the missed call message, you see more details about that call.

7. From here, you can add notes about the missed call. Click the trackball or trackpad, and choose Add Notes.

8. Another option on this screen is to call the person back. Click the trackball or trackpad, and choose Call.

9. You can also send the person an SMS or MMS from this same menu.

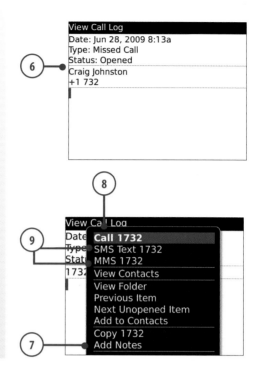

Making Free Calls with Your BlackBerry Curve

Some wireless carriers around the world support a technology called Unlicensed Mobile Access (UMA), also called Generic Access Network (GAN). This technology allows mobile phones that have Wi-Fi radios to seamlessly roam between the cellular network and Wi-Fi networks. This technology allows for certain benefits, including free phone calls.

How UMA Works

UMA has two parts. The first part is equipment that is installed at your wireless carrier. The second part is in your phone or BlackBerry. Your BlackBerry must have a Wi-Fi radio and the UMA software installed. In the case of the BlackBerry, your wireless carrier preloads this software if it supports UMA.

When your BlackBerry is in range of a Wi-Fi network and you have connected to that Wi-Fi network, your BlackBerry's connection to the wireless carrier disconnects from the cellular network and connects over the Internet via the

Wi-Fi hot spot. After that, all communications, including phone calls, go over the Wi-Fi network.

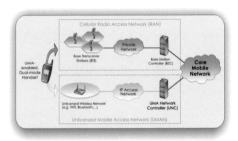

When you move between the regular cellular network and the Wi-Fi network, your call does not drop or stutter or give any other indication that you are moving between networks. If you start a call while connected to Wi-Fi and later move into the cellular network while still on that same call, the call remains free, as discussed next.

Benefits of UMA

The UMA technology has benefits. The first is to expand the reach of your wireless carrier's network. In areas that have low or no coverage, if you connect to a Wi-Fi network, that Wi-Fi network acts as another cell tower for your wireless carrier. This is very useful, especially in computer rooms where cell coverage normally is very bad or nonexistent, but it can also be handy in the basement of your home.

The second benefit of UMA is free calling. When your BlackBerry is connected to a Wi-Fi hot spot via UMA and you make a phone call, that phone call normally is free. We say normally because every carrier has different rules about how it implements UMA. Some require a small monthly fee to get the free calling, but that monthly fee can be offset by the fact that you can lower your regular monthly minute plan because many of your calls could be made while on Wi-Fi.

This free calling ability works regardless of whether you are in your home country. As long as you are connected to a Wi-Fi hot spot, your call is free. Imagine that you live in New York and you are sitting in a coffee shop in London. As long as you are connected to the coffee shop's Wi-Fi hot spot, your calls to the U.S. are all free. The ability for UMA to save you money is certainly there. Imagine how much money a company could save if it purchased its BlackBerry Curves from wireless carriers that support UMA.

Many wireless carriers around the world support UMA, including T-Mobile US, Rogers Wireless, and Orange, to name just a few. If your carrier does not support UMA, ask the carrier to look into it.

Which BlackBerry Curves Support UMA

The following BlackBerry Curves support UMA:

- BlackBerry Curve 8320
- BlackBerry Curve 8520
- BlackBerry Curve 8900

If you have one of these BlackBerry Curves, and your wireless carrier supports UMA, you should be all set. If your wireless carrier does not support UMA, these BlackBerry models will still work on that carrier, but you will have no UMA and no free calling.

>>>*step-by-step*

Setting Up UMA

The great thing about UMA is that it requires no setup and no special instructions for making calls while on Wi-Fi. The only setup that is needed is to associate your BlackBerry Curve with one or more Wi-Fi hot spots. As soon as your BlackBerry is aware of all the hot spots you normally come into contact with and knows how to connect to each one, it automatically switches to those networks when you are in range of them. As soon as Wi-Fi is established, UMA starts working automatically.

1. To associate with a Wi-Fi hot spot that includes your home Wi-Fi network, go to the Settings Folder on your BlackBerry, and click Set Up Wi-Fi.

2. The first time you run this setup wizard, you are shown some general information about Wi-Fi and UMA.

   If you do not want to see this information again, scroll down and check the box next to Don't show this introduction again.

3. Scroll down and click Next.

4. On the next screen, you see a list of choices. Click Scan For Networks to scan the area for Wi-Fi networks in range.

5. Your BlackBerry scans the airwaves for Wi-Fi networks in range.

6. After it completes its scan, which takes only a few seconds, you see a list of Wi-Fi networks in range. Click the Wi-Fi network you want to connect to.

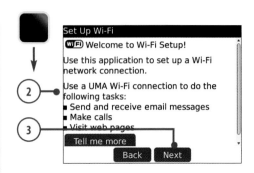

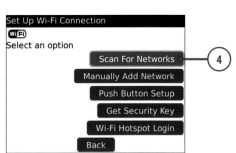

Note

If the Wi-Fi hot spot you are connecting to requires that you provide a username and password via its website, click the Wi-Fi Hotspot Login button.

This opens the hot spot browser and takes you to the hot spot's login screen, where you can type in the hot spot login information. This is typically used in hotels where the hotel provides you with this information at check-in. After you log in, this information is saved. The next time your BlackBerry is in range of this hot spot, it knows how to connect, and it automatically logs in for you.

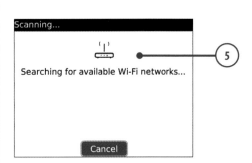

7. When you click that Wi-Fi net-work, if some kind of key is required, your BlackBerry prompts you. Enter the Wi-Fi network pass-word encryption key or pre-shared key to connect if required.

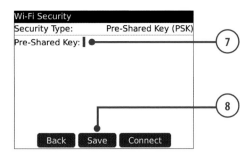

8. After you type in the required key, click Save.

9. The next screen asks you to save the Wi-Fi network profile. It pre-populates the profile name with the network name. Either leave the name as is or type in a new name such as Home or Work, and click Next.

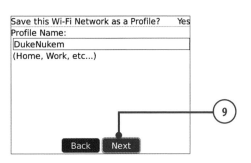

10. The final screen is a success screen.

Know the Wi-Fi Network Name

You need to know the Wi-Fi network name ahead of time. Normally coffee shops, airports, and other establish-ments can tell you the name of their Wi-Fi network. Often the name of that network gives away its location. If you are scanning at home, it is likely that you already know what your Wi-Fi network is called.

When you have successfully connected to the Wi-Fi hot spot, your BlackBerry Curve should connect to your carrier via UMA. As soon as you are connected to UMA, the regular signal meter on the top right of your BlackBerry screen should change to say UMA. The signal strength then reflects the signal strength of the Wi-Fi network. When you move out of Wi-Fi range, the signal meter changes back to showing GPRS or EDGE.

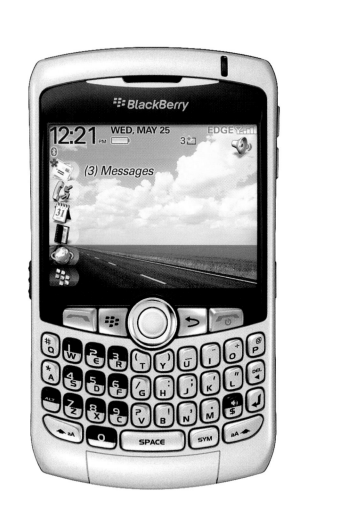

In this chapter, you learn how to work with your BlackBerry Curve's contacts. You learn how to customize the Contacts application and synchronize it with outside sources. Topics include the following:

→ Synchronizing your contacts with Windows or Mac

→ Synchronizing your contacts with online services

→ Adding custom ring tones to contacts

→ Working with contacts while on the go

Managing Contacts

Your contacts are probably the most important part of your life. They're certainly a central point on your BlackBerry Curve. You send email, Short Message Service (SMS) text messages, Multimedia Message Service (MMS) messages, and photos to your contacts. You also use your contacts to invite your friends to social networking sites such as Facebook, MySpace, and Twitter.

Knowing how to fully utilize the Contacts application on your BlackBerry Curve will increase your productivity and help you keep in touch more efficiently.

Getting Contacts onto Your BlackBerry Curve

Before you configure the Contacts application, you need to put some contacts into it. There are many ways to do this, from entering them manually to synchronizing them from your computer.

Synchronizing with a Windows Computer

If you are using a computer running Windows, you will use the BlackBerry Desktop Manager to synchronize your contacts. You should already have BlackBerry Desktop Manager installed if you followed the instructions in the Prologue. If you didn't, take a few minutes to follow those steps and install the BlackBerry Desktop Software.

1. Run the BlackBerry Desktop Manager, and connect your BlackBerry Curve to your computer using the USB cable.

2. Click Synchronize.

3. On the Synchronize screen, click the Synchronization menu item.

4. Click the Synchronization button next to Configure synchronization for my desktop program.

5. On the Intellisync Setup screen, click the check box next to Address Book, and click Setup.

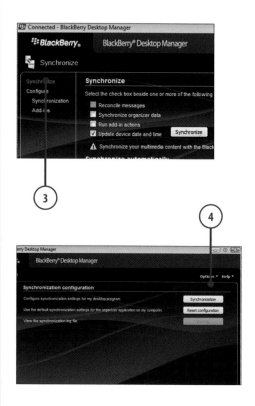

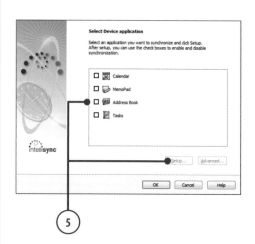

6. You are prompted to choose the desktop program you want to synchronize with. The selection list is based on what is actually installed. For now, choose Windows Address Book/Mail.

7. Click Two-way sync and click Next.

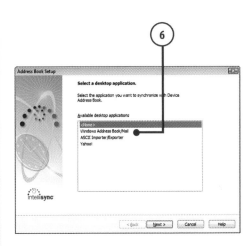

Synchronization Options Explained

The three synchronization options are Two-way sync, One-way sync from Device, and One-way sync to Device. If you think you will never edit or add contacts on your BlackBerry, and you're only doing this on your computer, select One-way sync to Device. If you prefer to make additions and changes only on your BlackBerry Curve and never on your computer, choose One-way sync from Device. Finally, if you are unsure, or you know that you could be making changes to contacts on both your BlackBerry Curve and computer, select Two-way sync. This option is the most common choice.

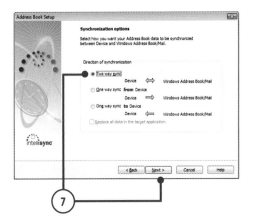

If you choose one of the One-way sync options, you can check the box next to Replace all data in the target application. This means that each time you synchronize, all the contact information on the target is erased and replaced.

8. On the last screen, click Finish.

>>>*step-by-step*

Customizing How the Contacts Are Synchronized

If you want to further customize how your contacts are synchronized, such as conflict resolution and filtering contacts, click the Advanced button on the Intellisync Setup screen.

1. Click the Conflict Resolution button.

More About Conflict Resolution

All these choices are valid only if you chose Two-way sync. Add all conflicting items tells Desktop Manager that if it sees that you modified the same contact on your BlackBerry and on your computer, it must keep both changes. This means that you will end up with duplicate entries, with each entry having slightly different information.

---

2. Click Cancel to return to the preceding screen.

3. Click the Filters button.

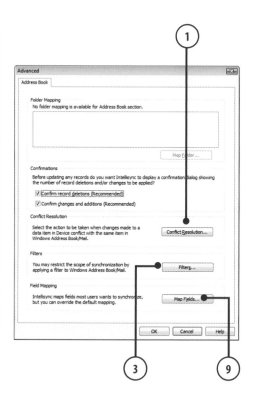

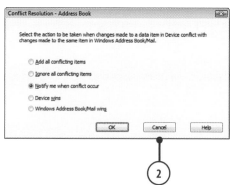

Conflicts Explained

Ignore all conflicting items tells
BlackBerry Manager that if it sees
a conflict, it must ignore that conflict and not synchronize the data.

Notify me when conflict occur
tells the BlackBerry Manager that
when it sees a conflict between
the BlackBerry Curve and your
computer, it must prompt you to
resolve the conflict.

Device wins tells the Desktop
Manager that if it sees a conflict
between your BlackBerry and
computer, it must assume that the
device (in this case, your
BlackBerry Curve) has the correct
information. It will then always
overwrite the address book entry
on the computer.

Windows Address Book/Mail wins
tells the Desktop Manager that in
the case of a conflict, the computer is always right, and the contact on the BlackBerry must be
overwritten with the one on the
computer.

4. On the Filters screen, click New,
   give the filter a name such as Test,
   and click OK.

5. To configure this filter, click the Field button to choose a contact field, such as Business State.

6. Click the Operator button to choose the condition, such as equals or contains. Then type the value into the Value field.

   For example, if you want to synchronize only contacts that have a Business State of New Jersey, you would select a field of Business State, an Operator of equals, and a Value of New Jersey.

7. After you have set up the filter, click the Add to List button. Each filter can have multiple filter conditions, so you can then repeat the steps but select different fields.

8. For now, click the Cancel button to return to the preceding screen, and then click Cancel again to return to the screen before that.

9. Click the Map Fields button. (See page 76.)

   If you've ever wanted to change the field mappings between your computer and your BlackBerry Curve, this is where you make those changes. Scroll through this list for future reference.

10. Click the Cancel button twice to return to the Intellisync Setup screen, and then click OK.

11. Click Synchronize on the top left to return to the main Synchronization screen.

To synchronize with your BlackBerry Curve right away, click the Synchronize button.

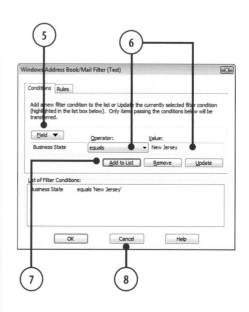

Use this screen to change field mappings

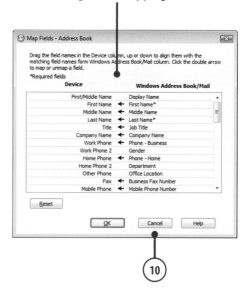

Synchronizing with an Apple Mac

If you are using an Apple Mac, you can use either PocketMac for BlackBerry or Missing Sync for BlackBerry to synchronize your contacts. You should already have one of these installed if you followed the steps in the Prologue, but if not, take a few minutes to follow those steps and install PocketMac for BlackBerry or Missing Sync for BlackBerry.

The Official Mac Solution for BlackBerry

After we completed writing this book, RIM released the BlackBerry Desktop Manager for the Apple Mac. Unfortunately, it was too late to include it in this book; however, we have an on-line article that covers all the features of this new application. So if you don't like the choices below, head over to http://www.MyBlackBerryCurve.info to read all about BlackBerry Desktop Manager for OS X.

>>>*step-by-step*

PocketMac for BlackBerry

We discuss PocketMac for BlackBerry first.

1. Run PocketMac for BlackBerry. Connect your BlackBerry Curve to the computer using the included micro-USB or mini-USB cable.

2. Click the picture of the BlackBerry to configure PocketMac for BlackBerry.

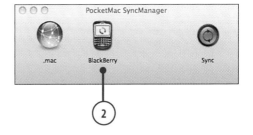

3. Click Contacts.

4. Click the check box next to Sync Contacts Between the BlackBerry and Mac.

5. Put a check mark next to the application that you want to synchronize your contacts with.

    You have a number of choices, depending on which applications you have installed on your Mac.

    Choose AddressBookContacts for now. You can come back and change it later.

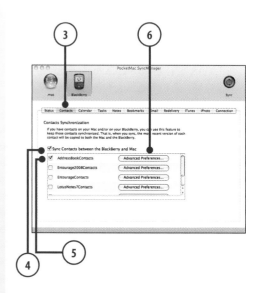

6. Click the Advanced Preferences button.

7. The first choice you can make on the Advanced Preferences screen is between synchronizing contacts in all categories in your Address Book, or selected categories. There may be a situation where you want only personal contacts or business contacts on your BlackBerry. On the BlackBerry, groupings of contacts are called Categories, but on the Mac they are called Groups. If you want to limit which groups of contacts are synchronized to your BlackBerry Curve, click Sync Only Categories Selected Below, and put check marks next to the groups you want to synchronize.

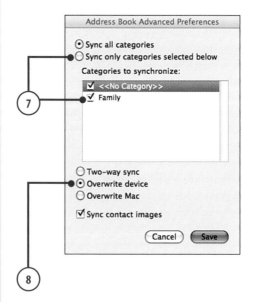

8. The next choice is how the synchronization occurs. The default choice is Two-way sync. Two-way sync means that PocketMac for BlackBerry compares the contacts on your BlackBerry Curve and on your Mac to see which one has

the more recent changes. It then synchronizes the newer version of the contact.

Overwrite device tells PocketMac for BlackBerry to overwrite all contacts on your BlackBerry with the contacts on your Mac. This option is useful if you have decided to make changes to your contacts only on your Mac, and you will never make changes to contacts on your BlackBerry. If you choose this option, you must remember that if you modify a contact or add a new contact on your BlackBerry, it will be overwritten when you synchronize.

Overwrite Mac tells PocketMac for BlackBerry to overwrite all contacts on your Mac with the contacts on your BlackBerry. This option is useful if you have decided to make changes to your contacts only on your BlackBerry, and you will never make changes to contacts on your Mac. If you choose this option, you must remember that if you modify a contact or add a contact on your Mac, it will be overwritten when you synchronize.

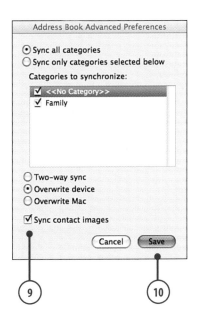

9.   At the bottom of the screen is a check box next to Sync Contact Images. When you check this, PocketMac for BlackBerry includes any contact images that you have added to contacts either on your BlackBerry Curve or Mac.

10. After you have made your choices, click the Save button.

To synchronize your BlackBerry Curve right away, click the Sync icon.

>>>*step-by-step*

Missing Sync for BlackBerry

Next we cover synchronizing using Missing Sync for BlackBerry.

1. Run Missing Sync for BlackBerry, and then connect your BlackBerry Curve to the computer using the included micro-USB or mini-USB cable.

   After your initial synchronization via cable, Missing Sync for BlackBerry can synchronize your BlackBerry via Bluetooth as soon as it detects it is in range. For many people this is a very convenient option.

2. Put a check mark next to Contacts. You then can set up how the Contacts synchronize to your BlackBerry Curve.

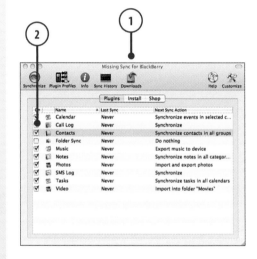

Synchronization Explained

If you select Synchronize, Missing Sync for BlackBerry performs a two-way sync. This means that it compares the contacts on your BlackBerry Curve with the contacts on your Mac and synchronizes the newest contacts from the one to the other. If it sees two contacts with slightly different data, it prompts you to resolve the conflict.

Overwrite device with desktop data on next sync only tells Missing Sync for BlackBerry to erase and overwrite the contacts on your BlackBerry Curve the next time it synchronizes and to resume two-way synchronizations after that.

Always overwrite device with desktop data tells Missing Sync for BlackBerry to always erase and overwrite your BlackBerry Curve's contacts with the ones on your Mac. Remember that if you choose this option, if you add or modify contacts on your BlackBerry, the next time you syn-chronize, they will be erased and overwritten.

3. Under the heading Contact Settings are the three choices described above.

4. Below the Contact Settings are two Synchronize options. If you select All Contacts, Missing Sync for BlackBerry always synchro-nizes all contacts, no matter what group they are in. If you do not want to synchronize all contacts but rather contacts in specific groups such as Family or Work, choose Selected Groups. After that, select which groups you want to synchronize. Remember that groups on your Mac are called categories on your BlackBerry.

5. Click OK to return to the previous screen.

>>> Go Further

SYNCHRONIZING WITH LINUX

Linux also has options to synchronize your BlackBerry. They are not officially supported by Research In Motion (RIM), but they do work. We do not walk you through the steps, but we will direct you to a useful link that describes how to use different tools such as Barry, Evolution, and OpenSync: http://www.progweb.com/modules/blackberry/index-en.html.

Creating Contacts on the Go

You can create new contacts or modify contacts while on the go in a number of ways. This is likely the most common way you will add contacts to your BlackBerry Curve. After all, it is a device to be used while out of the house or office.

>>>*step-by-step*

Manually Entering Contact Information

Follow these steps to add contact information by hand:

1. From the BlackBerry Home Screen, click the Contacts icon.

2. If the cursor is at the top of the list of contacts, click Add Contact.

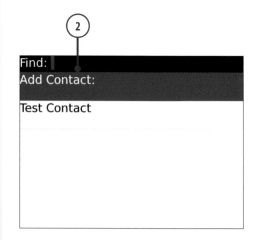

3. If the cursor is not at the top of the list of contacts, click the Menu button, and choose New Contact.

4. Enter the contact's information on this screen.

5. Click the Escape button to exit.

6. Choose Save when prompted.

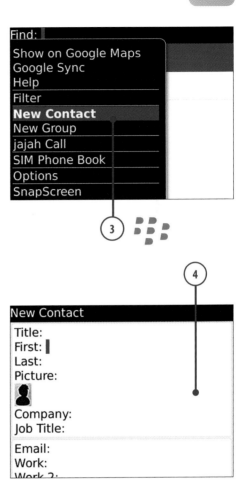

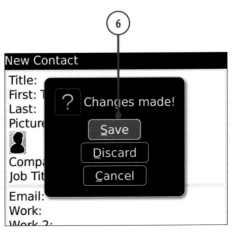

Adding a Contact from an Email

You also can add contact information from an email message.

1. Scroll up to the From or CC field, and scroll over the name you want to add to your contacts.

2. Click the trackball or trackpad, and choose Add to Contacts.

Note
If you do not see Add to Contacts, it means that this person is already in your Address Book.

---

3. Modify any of the information that is automatically imported into the new contact.

4. Click the Escape button to exit.

5. Choose Save when prompted.

Importing a vCard

vCard stands for VersitCard, a universal standard format for sending business cards. These vCards can contain all kinds of contact information, including pictures and even audio clips. If someone attaches their vCard to an email, you can import that vCard into your Address Book right from your BlackBerry Curve.

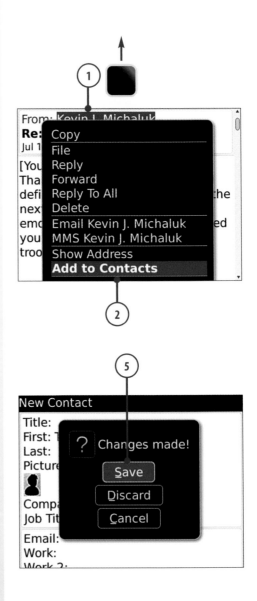

1. If someone emails you his or her vCard, scroll to the bottom of the email until the cursor is on the vCard, which looks like a small open book with the person's name next to it.

2. Click the trackball or trackpad, and choose Add to Contacts.

My Podcasts:-
CrackBerry: http://crackberry.com/crack-team/podcasts
MCA: http://mca.libsyn.com
BB4Biz: http://blackberry.libsyn.com
Capital 604: http://www.capital604.com/audio/PodCasts/
(Sent from GMail - GBs of free email)

📖 Craig Johnston

(1)

It's Not All Good

NOT THE FULL VCARD

The vCard that you open on your BlackBerry is a stripped-down version of the actual vCard. The BlackBerry service does not send the entire vCard, just certain fields of it. So when you get back to your desktop email program, you can import the vCard into it, which will eventually update the contact on your BlackBerry. The portion of the vCard that is sent contains the fields you need, such as name, address, company name, phone numbers, and email addresses. Fields such as the picture field are unavailable.

Working with Contacts

You can work with the contacts on your BlackBerry Curve, including deleting existing contacts, editing contacts, and adding a picture or ring tone for a contact.

>>>step-by-step

Deleting a Contact

Follow these steps to delete a contact:

1. From the BlackBerry Home Screen, click the Contacts icon.

2. Scroll to the contact you want to delete, or start typing the person's name to automatically filter the display.

3. After the contact is selected, click the Menu button, and choose Delete.

4. Choose Delete in the confirmation dialog box.

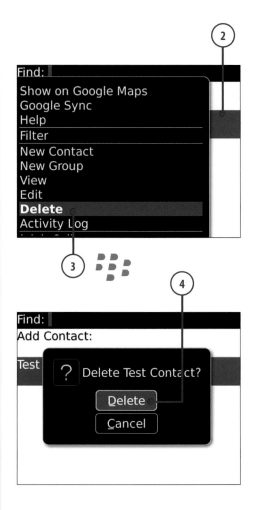

>>>step-by-step

Editing a Contact

Follow these steps to edit a contact:

1. From the BlackBerry Home Screen, click the Contacts icon.

2. Scroll to the contact you want to edit, or start typing the person's name to automatically filter the display.

3. After the contact is selected, click the Menu button, and choose Edit.

4. Make your edits, and click the Escape button to exit.

5. Choose Save when prompted.

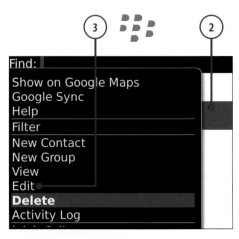

Adding a Picture for One of Your Contacts

Follow these steps to add a contact's picture (the first 3 steps are identical to Editing a Contact):

1. From the BlackBerry Home Screen, click the Contacts icon.

2. Scroll to the contact you want to add a picture to, or start typing the person's name.

3. After the contact is selected, click the Menu button, and choose Edit.

4. Scroll over the picture, click the trackball or trackpad, and choose Add Picture.

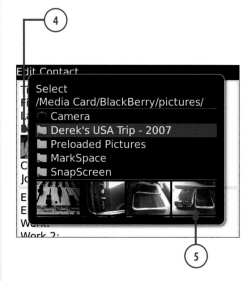

Taking a Picture of Your Contact

If you do not have a picture for this person yet, scroll up to Camera when you see the list of pictures on your BlackBerry. Your BlackBerry starts the camera, allowing you to take a picture. After you do so, you see the Edit window.

5. You see a new window showing all the pictures on your BlackBerry.

6. After you choose the picture you want, you see a new window, allowing you to edit the portion of the picture you want to use as the contact's picture.

7. Start by using the trackball or trackpad to move the crop area around.

8. If you need to zoom in or out, click the trackball or trackpad and choose Zoom. You then see the Zoom slider appear on the left of the screen.

9. Use the trackball or trackpad to zoom in or out.

10. When you are satisfied with the zoom level, click the trackball or trackpad.

11. If you need to, again move the crop area around with the trackball or trackpad.

12. When you are satisfied with the area to be cropped and used as the picture, click the trackball or trackpad and choose Crop and Save.

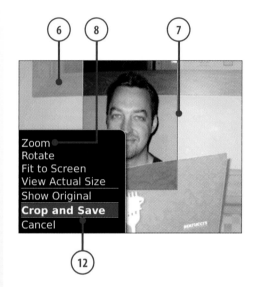

Adding a Custom Ring Tone for One of Your Contacts

Follow these steps to add a special ring tone for a contact:

1. From the BlackBerry Home Screen, click the Contacts icon.

2. Scroll to the contact you want to add a ring tone to, or start typing the person's name.

3. Click the trackball or trackpad, and choose Add Custom Ring Tone.

4. When you make this choice, a new field is created at the bottom of the contact called Custom Ring Tone.

5. Click Browse to see a list of the ring tones you already have stored on your BlackBerry. When you find the Ring Tone you want to use, click to select it.

6. Scroll all the way to the top of the list of ring tones to see ring tones you have added.

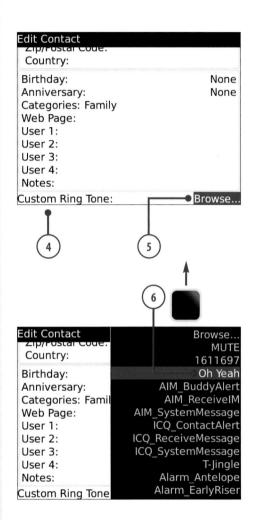

Configuring the Contacts Application

There may be some things you want to change about how the Contacts application works on your BlackBerry Curve.

>>>*step-by-step*

Changing How the Contacts Application Works

Follow these steps to adjust the Contacts application:

1. Open Contacts from the BlackBerry Home Screen.

2. Press the Menu button and choose Options. The two categories are General Options and Desktop. With General Options, you can change settings that affect the Contacts application. With Desktop, you can change settings relevant only to the Desktop synchronization. If you have a corporate BlackBerry, you see the Desktop category even though you may be synchronizing your contacts wirelessly.

3. Click General Options.

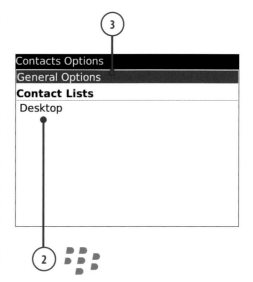

4. Under General Options, you can change the sort order of your contacts by modifying the Sort By field. Your choices are First Name, Last Name, and Company.

5. The next option is Separators. You can change this to None, Stripes, or Lines. This changes how the Contact List is displayed—with no separator, separated by lines, or with contacts listed with alternating-color stripes as a background.

6. The next option is Allow Duplicate Names. Setting this option to No prevents duplicate names in your Contacts application when you synchronize from multiple sources. Unfortunately, you must leave this set to Yes if you sync with Google, as covered in the next section.

7. Last is Confirm Delete. Setting this to No allows you to delete a contact without having to confirm that's what you want to do.

8. Press the Escape button to go back to the main Contacts Options screen.

9. Scroll to Desktop and select it.

10. The first option is Wireless Synchronization. If you have a personal BlackBerry, this says Not Available, and the option cannot be changed. If you have a company BlackBerry, you can set this to Yes or No. Setting it to No stops the wireless synchronization of your contacts.

11. The second option on this screen is actually not an option but rather an indication of how many contacts you have.

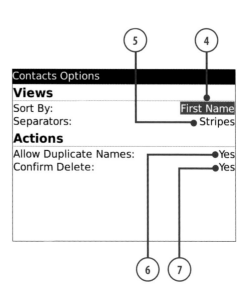

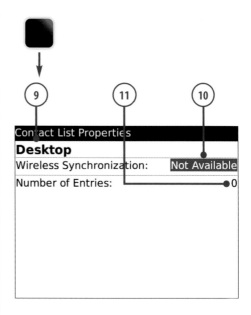

Synchronizing Contacts with Online Services

Many online services allow you to synchronize your BlackBerry contacts with your account online. This is normally done via a Desktop Manager Add-In, which means you need to synchronize your online contacts while connected to a computer. But sometimes the online service provides a way to synchronize your BlackBerry contacts wirelessly. One such service is Google Sync, which wirelessly synchronizes your Gmail contacts and Google Calendar with your BlackBerry.

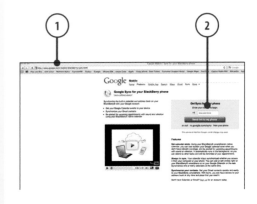

>>>*step-by-step*

Synchronizing with Google

The first step of getting your BlackBerry set up to synchronize wirelessly with Google is to install the Google Sync application on your BlackBerry. Luckily, this can also be done over the air.

1. From your desktop computer, visit the Google Sync website at http://www.google.com/mobile/blackberry/sync.html.

2. Type the phone number of your BlackBerry Curve, and click Send link to my phone. Google sends you an SMS that contains a link to install the application wirelessly.

3. When the SMS arrives on your BlackBerry Curve, open it and click the link. You are taken to a mobile-friendly web page with a link to install the application.

4. Click Install Now to start the installation. Your BlackBerry shows you information about the application.

5. Click the Download button.

6. After the application installs, a dialog box states that the application has successfully installed. Click Run to start Google Sync.

7. The first screen asks you to type in your Google username and password. Type them in and click Next.

8. You should be taken to the Options screen next.

9. To synchronize your Google Contacts with your BlackBerry Contacts, check the box next to Sync Contacts.

10. You can change the synchronization interval by clicking the When To Sync setting. The default is Automatic, but you can set it to Manual. When you set it to Manual, you have to manually start the synchronization process by running Google Sync, clicking the trackball or touchpad, and choosing Sync Now.

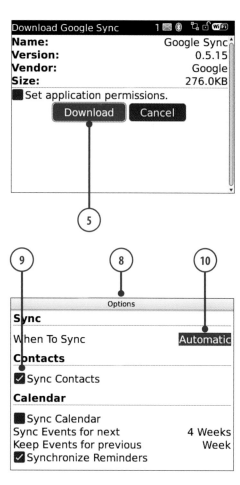

Duplicate Names

If you try to synchronize your Contacts and you see a screen that says "Your phone settings are preventing Google Sync from syncing your contacts...", you need to configure your contacts on your BlackBerry to allow duplicate names, as discussed in the preceding section.

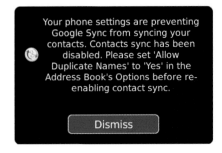

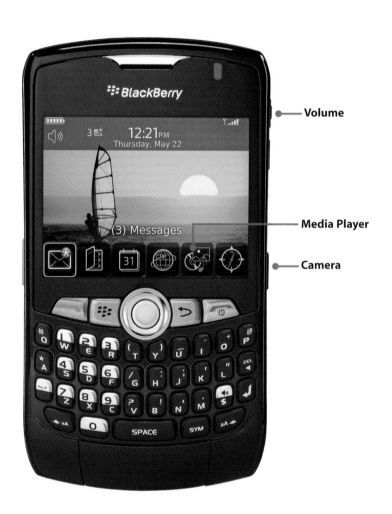

Volume

Media Player

Camera

In this chapter, you learn about the multi-media capabilities of your BlackBerry Curve and how you can synchronize multimedia files to and from a PC or Mac. Topics include the following:

3

→ Synchronizing with iTunes and Windows Media
→ Working with multimedia files using Roxio Media Manager
→ Playing audio and video on your BlackBerry Curve
→ Recording video and taking pictures

Listening to Audio and Watching Video

Many people buy the BlackBerry Curve for its multimedia capabilities. Being able to watch videos and play music while on the go is an attractive feature, and we will cover how to do just that.

Using Roxio Media Manager (Windows)

Before you can watch those videos and listen to that music, you have to get them onto your BlackBerry Curve. When you download the BlackBerry Desktop Software, you can choose to download it with or without the Roxio Media Manager. Earlier we suggested that you download and install the BlackBerry Desktop Software with Roxio Media Manager. If you have not done so, please follow the earlier instructions on downloading and installing the BlackBerry Desktop Software with Roxio Media Manager.

Roxio Media Manager is a special version of the Media Manager application that integrates with the BlackBerry. It allows you to move audio and video to and from your BlackBerry. It can automatically convert the media on-the-fly so that it fits the BlackBerry screen better and is smaller in size while retaining the quality.

>>>step-by-step

Working with Roxio Media Manager

1. To start moving multimedia files to your BlackBerry, run the BlackBerry Desktop Manager, connect your BlackBerry Curve to your computer via the USB cable, and click Media in the BlackBerry Desktop Manager.

2. On the Media Screen, click Media Manager to launch Roxio Media Manager.

3. The first time you click Media, you are asked to agree to an End User License Agreement (EULA). Roxio Media Manager then starts.

4. The first time Roxio Media Manager starts, it asks you if it should scan your computer for multimedia files and automatically make them available. It is a good idea to do this, because it will save you time later. However, if you do not want to or are unsure, click Remind Me Later.

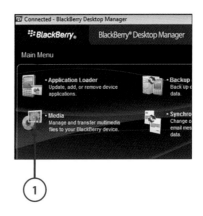

>>>*step-by-step*

Configuring Roxio Media Manager

Before we get to moving files to your BlackBerry Curve, you should configure Roxio Media Manager so that it handles these files the way you want it to.

1. Click Tools, Options to bring up the Roxio Media Manager options. Make sure the BlackBerry tab is selected.

2. The first option is for Photo Files. This allows you to configure what Roxio Media Manager does when it moves photos to your BlackBerry. For the best quality, set Photo file type to As is. This tells the software to leave the photo unchanged when it moves it to your BlackBerry. If you have a media card in your BlackBerry, you should leave this option set to As is.

Note

If you do not have a media card in your BlackBerry Curve, you may want to set the Photo file type to jpg and set the Photo size to something that is closest to your BlackBerry Curve's screen size. The screen sizes are as follows:

- BlackBerry Curve 8300: 320×240
- BlackBerry Curve 8500: 320×240
- BlackBerry Curve 8900: 480×360

Setting the options this way means that you can fit many more photos onto your BlackBerry. Because you are reducing the photos' size to be as close as possible to the BlackBerry Curve's screen size, you can enjoy them on your BlackBerry. But if you send them to someone else (covered later), they may appear quite small on that person's computer screen. This is still a great option for saving space if you have no media card inserted.

3. The next option is Video Files. This allows you to configure what Roxio Media Manager does when it moves video files to your BlackBerry.

By default, the Video file type is set to mp4, and the Resizing is set to Maintain Aspect Ratio.

The other setting is Video size / resolution. This is set to Best Quality Video - largest file size.

Whether or not you have a media card inserted into your BlackBerry Curve, it is best to leave this option set as is. This tells Roxio Media Manager to convert the video to mp4 format, keep the video's aspect ratio when it resizes it, and, when it compresses it using mp4, to produce the best-quality video.

It is unlikely that you will set Roxio to leave the video as is, because it may not have the correct aspect ratio, or it might be too large.

The Video size / resolution setting is where you set the size that the video will be converted to. This is not the size on disk or in memory, but rather the screen size.

4. The last option on the screen is Audio Files. This tells Roxio what to do with audio files that you have on your computer.

The three settings are Audio format, Audio Sample Rate, and Audio bitrate. By default, the Audio format is set to As is. This tells Roxio not to convert the audio files to another format.

The choices for Audio format are mp3 and aac.

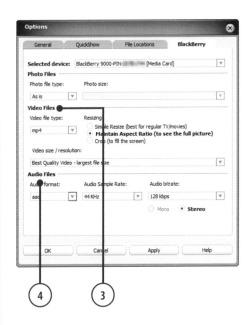

Note

Video compression is a technique that goes through a video frame by frame, trying to compress the amount of space it takes up on a disk or in memory. It does this using a number of methods, including looking for parts of frames that are static and parts that are repeated often. In this instance the video is also reduced in screen size so that it fits on your BlackBerry Curve's screen.

Note

MP3 stands for MPEG-1 Audio Layer 3. It is the most common compression technique used to reduce the size of audio files. It reduces the size that an audio file takes up in memory or on a disk but preserves the audio quality as close to the original as possible.

AAC stands for Advanced Audio Coding. AAC is an audio compression technique that was designed as a successor to MP3. It typically produces higher-quality audio than MP3 while compressing the audio files to the same size as MP3 does. AAC is used heavily by Apple but is not exclusive to Apple and is freely available to everyone.

Note

One thing to remember about audio compression is that when you compress an audio file, in most cases you reduce the quality of that audio. Although most ears cannot pick up that loss in audio quality, it still happens. If you take an uncompressed audio file that is at its highest quality and compress it once, you get audio loss. If you take that compressed audio file and compress it again, you will get more audio loss. The more you recompress an audio file, the worse it sounds.

This information is important to remember when you decide what to do with audio files when Roxio sends them to your BlackBerry Curve. If you know that all your audio files are in WAV format (which is uncompressed), you will likely choose the Audio format MP3 or AAC. Both of these choices tell Roxio to compress the audio before sending it to your BlackBerry. However, if your audio files are all MP3 or AAC, it would be inadvisable to set the Audio format to MP3 or AAC, because this tells Roxio to compress the audio. This would mean that the audio would be compressed twice, further reducing its quality.

It is probably best to leave the audio settings at their defaults if you are unsure what the source of your audio will be. In reality it is highly likely that all the audio files on your computer have already been compressed to either MP3 or AAC, so leaving the default values would preserve the audio's quality.

Note

One more thing about AAC files: If you purchase audio on iTunes, your audio files are saved in AAC format. The files are actually saved as MPEG-4 files, but AAC is the core of the audio compression used in MPEG-4 (or MP4), so the filenames end in .m4a, which stands for MPEG-4 Audio. Because AAC allows files to contain Digital Rights Management (DRM), which allows a seller to restrict who can listen to those audio files, if you purchase audio in iTunes and it is not DRM-free, those files are not copied to your BlackBerry Curve. This is because those audio files can be played only on computers, iPods, and iPhones that are registered to you. If you later convert your iTunes music to iTunes Plus music that is DRM-free, you can move those files to your BlackBerry.

5. If you click the General tab of the Options screen, you see two settings.

Don't warn me when rotating photos tells Roxio not to display a warning message when rotating photos.

When you rotate a photo in Roxio, you slightly reduce its quality, because it takes your photo that is already compressed using JPEG (jpg), rotates it, and saves it again to the JPEG format, which compresses it again. If you do not mind this recompression or slight loss in picture quality, check this box. You can ignore the second option.

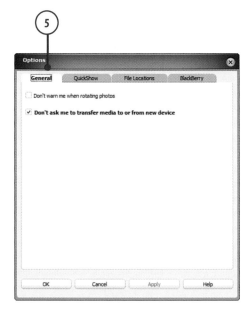

6. If you click the QuickShow tab, you can adjust how QuickShow displays your pictures when you select QuickShow.

You can use QuickShow by selecting multiple photos in Roxio, right-clicking, and choosing QuickShow. This starts the QuickShow slide show.

7. If you click the File Locations tab, you can change where Roxio saves your media files on your computer when it moves or copies them from your BlackBerry.

Note

Watching Folders is a feature of Roxio Media Manager that is worth taking a look at before we continue. The idea of telling Roxio to watch folders is a way of automating the task of moving multimedia files to the Roxio Media Library. From there, you can select them and copy or move them to your BlackBerry. After you set it up and enable it, Roxio starts a small service each time you start Windows. This service watches the directories you tell it to. When it sees new files appear in that directory, it immediately places these files in the Roxio Media Library in preparation for the next time you connect your BlackBerry. Using this technique, you do not have to remember which files you may or may not have moved to your Media Library.

For example, if you typically save your pictures into a specific folder on your computer, and you want your BlackBerry Curve to always have those same pictures, you would set that folder as a watched folder. The same goes for video files, music files, or even regular documents such as Microsoft Word and PDF files.

8. To set up folder watching, from the main Media Manager screen, click Tools.

9. Select Watched Folders.

10. Roxio may have already prepopulated this list with folders that it thinks you want to synchronize.

11. You can remove a folder it has selected by clicking the folder and then clicking the Remove Folder button.

12. To remove all the folders, click the Clear All button.

13. Click the Add Folder button to choose new folders that you want Roxio to watch.

14. When all your folders are selected, make sure you check the box next to Start Folder Watching. This tells Roxio that you want to start watching these folders for changes.

15. At the bottom of the screen are three check boxes. Watch folders at startup tells Roxio that you want to start a small service when Windows starts that continually watches these folders.

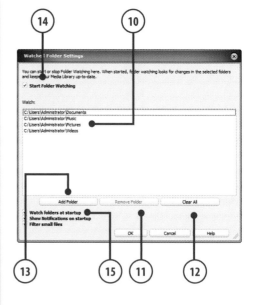

It's Not All Good

Unfortunately, this feature does not automatically copy the new files to your BlackBerry. It would be great if it did, because that would really make this a true hands-off solution. However, this is not the case right now.

>>>step-by-step

Using Roxio Media Manager

Now to the main reason to use Roxio Media Manager—to move that media to your BlackBerry Curve. On the main screen of Roxio Media Manager are three icons—Manage Pictures, Manage Music, and Manage Videos.

Each of these icons opens the Media Manager screen and selects the specific category of media. For example, if you click Manage Music, you see the Manage Media screen, and Music is selected.

Your BlackBerry Curve

Your BlackBerry Curve's Media Card

Note

Before we continue, we should discuss how the Media Manager works. When you first start Roxio Media Manager, it asks if you want it to scan your computer and find media. If you say yes, it does so. When it finds media on your computer, it catalogs it in the Media Library. Your pictures, music, and videos remain on your computer in the same place they were before, but Media Manager creates a catalog or library of that media so that you can easily search it and manipulate it.

When you see the Media Manager main screen, you are looking at the Media Library. The library is broken into media types such as Pictures, Video, Music, Documents, Playlists, and Voice Notes.

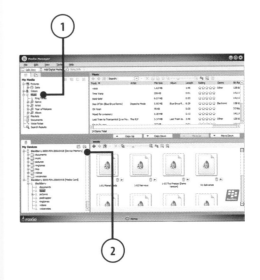

1. You can expand each media type to see how the library has further categorized it. For example, if you expand the Music type, you see that Roxio has categorized your music into Genre, Artist, and so on. This helps you find what you are looking for more quickly, especially when your library grows very large and you have hundreds or thousands of music files.

To move or copy media to your BlackBerry Curve, you must first select where that media must be moved or copied. The Manage Media screen is split in two, with your BlackBerry on the bottom and your Media Library on top.

2. If you expand the display by clicking the + to the left of your BlackBerry Curve, you see the different folders on your BlackBerry. You see folders for Music, Video, Pictures, and Documents. If your BlackBerry Curve has a media card inserted (this would be a Micro-SD card), you see this on the screen.

Note

If you do have a media card installed, it is highly recommended that you move or copy your media files to the media card and not the actual BlackBerry. This is because the media card has much more memory than your BlackBerry. If you fill up the memory on your BlackBerry with media, your BlackBerry may become slow. So it is always best to put your media on the media card.

Of course, if you do not have a media card, you must put your media on your BlackBerry. If you are in this situation, try to reduce the amount of space that the media takes up by configuring Roxio Media Manager to compress the files as much as possible, as discussed earlier.

3. If you expand the display under the media card, you see more folders, and again you see folders for Music, Videos, Pictures, and Documents.

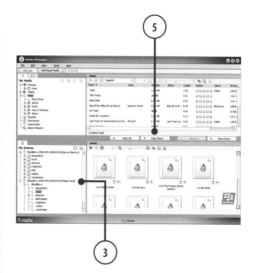

4. When you have found the media files you want to copy or move to your BlackBerry, simply select them. To select multiple files that are not next to each other, hold down the Ctrl key and click each file you want to move or copy. Release the Ctrl key after you select the last file. If you want to copy or move many files that are next to each other, click the first file, and then hold down the spacebar and click the last file.

5. The next decision you need to make is whether you want to just put a copy of the files on your BlackBerry or move them off your computer onto your BlackBerry. It is probably better to copy the files rather than move them, but it is up to you.

If you want to copy the files to your BlackBerry, make sure that you have selected where those files must be copied to on your BlackBerry, and click the Copy Down button.

6. You are prompted with a message asking if you want to Convert for Optimal Playback, Copy with no Conversion, or Advanced Conversion Options.

The Copy with no Conversion choice is selected by default. You probably made these choices earlier, when you configured Roxio Media Manager, but Media Manager prompts you again in case you changed your mind.

7. For now, leave the default choice, and click OK. The files are copied to your BlackBerry Curve.

Using BlackBerry Media Sync (Windows)

Although you can use Roxio Media Manager to organize and synchronize all your multimedia, you may already be using Apple's iTunes. If this is the case, you have a solution that will synchronize your music from iTunes to your BlackBerry Curve. The product you would use is called BlackBerry Media Sync.

Setting Up Media Sync

BlackBerry Media Sync is specifically designed to synchronize your music from iTunes. It does not handle video files such as movies and TV shows that you may already have in iTunes. For those, you still need to use the Roxio Media Manager.

>>>*step-by-step*

1. To set up and use BlackBerry Media Sync, close the Roxio Media Manager. You are returned to the BlackBerry Desktop Manager's Media screen.

2. On the right of this screen, click the Start button to launch BlackBerry Media Sync.

3. If you have not already installed BlackBerry Media Sync, you are prompted to do so. If you accept, BlackBerry Media Sync is downloaded and installed. After it has been installed, click BlackBerry Media Sync again to launch it.

4. The first time you run BlackBerry Media Sync, you see a Welcome screen, which is actually a setup screen.

5. The first field is called Name your device. It is prepopulated with BlackBerry Curve, and in parentheses is your BlackBerry's PIN. You can overwrite this with anything you like.

6. The next field is Music location. If you have a media card inserted in your BlackBerry Curve, it defaults to the media card and shows its size.

7. The next field is Keep this amount of memory free. This field defaults to 10%. This tells Media Sync to leave at least 10% of the memory free when it synchronizes your music.

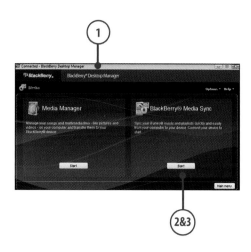

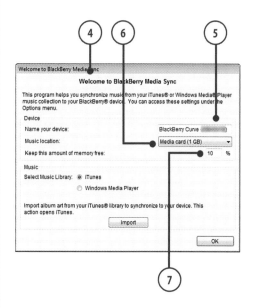

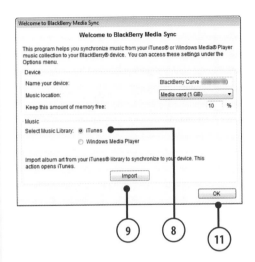

8. The second section on the Welcome screen is Music. The only field is Select Music Library. This allows you to select where the music comes from.

    Your choices are iTunes for Apple iTunes and Windows Media Player. Both of these applications build their own libraries of music and let you create playlists. Media Sync can synchronize playlists from either. At this point you should choose either iTunes or Windows Media Player.

Note

It is highly recommended that you always put multimedia files on the media card. If you do not want to, however, you can click the drop-down field and choose your BlackBerry Curve. If you do not have a media card, you must leave the location set to your BlackBerry Curve.

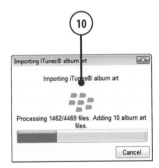

9. If you choose iTunes, click the Import button. This imports all your album art from your iTunes library so that when a song is sent to your BlackBerry Curve, the album art is sent along with it.

10. When you click Import, iTunes opens, and you see the Importing iTunes album art screen.

11. Click OK to see the main BlackBerry Media Sync screen.

Note

Leaving memory free is always a good idea. It is even more important when you do not have a media card and you are using your BlackBerry Curve's main memory for your music.

12. This screen shows your BlackBerry Curve and, next to it, a graphical representation of your memory.

The percentage of used space in yellow is the amount of memory used by other content. The percentage of space taken up by playlists that have been synchronized using Media Sync is shown in gray. The percentage free space is shown in black.

13. On the lower half of the screen you see your playlists.

These are playlists that you have previously created in either iTunes or Windows Media Player.

In Media Sync, you can only select which playlists to send to your BlackBerry Curve; you cannot create them.

14. After you have put check marks next to the playlist or playlists you want to send to your BlackBerry Curve, you are almost ready to synchronize.

15. Before you synchronize, right next to the large Sync button you see Add random music to free space.

If you put a check mark next to this, Media Sync synchronizes the playlists you selected. If any free space is left, Media Sync adds random songs to your BlackBerry Curve. This can be fun, because it is a surprise to see what music has been chosen for you.

16. When you are ready to synchronize, click the Sync button.

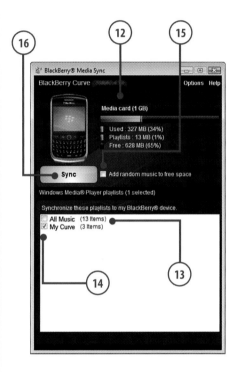

Note

If you need to create a new playlist, exit Media Sync, start either iTunes or Windows Media Player, and create a new playlist. Then drag the music from your library into that playlist to populate it with music.

17. After Media Sync has finished synchronizing, unplug your BlackBerry Curve, run the Media Player on your BlackBerry, choose Music, and then Playlists. You should see your newly synchronized playlist.

Along with the playlist, the actual music has been synchronized to your BlackBerry Curve. So if you want to play a specific song, escape from Playlists and go to either All Songs, Artists, Albums, or Genres to find the song.

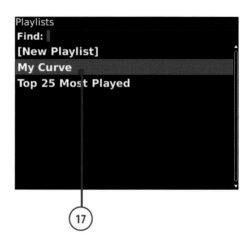

Using PocketMac and Missing Sync for BlackBerry (Mac OS X)

If you are an Apple Mac user running OS X, you can use two applications to synchronize multimedia to and from your BlackBerry—PocketMac for BlackBerry and Missing Sync for Blackberry. We cover both applications in this chapter.

The Official Mac Solution for BlackBerry

After we completed writing this book, RIM released the BlackBerry Desktop Manager for the Apple Mac. Unfortunately, it was too late to include it in this book; however, we have an on-line article that covers all the features of this new application. So if you don't like the choices below, head over to http://www.MyBlackBerryCurve.info to read all about BlackBerry Desktop Manager for OS X.

>>>step-by-step

PocketMac for BlackBerry

We discussed this application in the Prologue, so you should have it installed already. If not, please take a few minutes to follow the installation instructions for PocketMac for BlackBerry in the Prologue.

1. When you have PocketMac for BlackBerry installed and running, connect your BlackBerry Curve to your Mac via the USB cable.

2. When you are prompted to turn on Mass Storage Mode, choose Yes.

Note

Mass Storage Mode allows your BlackBerry Curve's media card to be seen as a Volume on your Mac. If your BlackBerry is on your company's BES, this feature might have been disabled for security reasons, and unfortunately you will not be able to synchronize your music.

---

3. In PocketMac for BlackBerry, click the BlackBerry icon to see the settings.

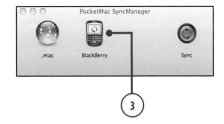

4. Click the iTunes tab. This tab allows you to select one or more playlists from iTunes and copy or "push" those playlists and their music to your BlackBerry Curve.

5. Check the box next to Push iTunes Music to the BlackBerry from the Mac.

6. Put a check mark next to the playlists you want to be pushed to your BlackBerry.

7. To synchronize your music to your BlackBerry Curve, click the green Sync button on the top right of the window.

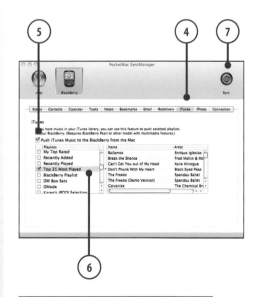

Note

PocketMac for BlackBerry does not allow you to create new playlists; it can only synchronize existing playlists. If you need to create a new playlist, close PocketMac for BlackBerry, open iTunes, and create one or more new playlists. Drag the songs you want to those playlists. When your playlists are ready, run PocketMac for BlackBerry again, return to this screen, and choose those playlists.

It's Not All Good

If you want to copy videos to your BlackBerry Curve, unfortunately PocketMac for BlackBerry cannot do this. You need to purchase a copy of Missing Sync for BlackBerry, which has a built-in video conversion feature. Or you can use another program to convert your videos to a format that is suitable for your BlackBerry. Many programs on the marketplace can do these video conversions. Some are free, and others are not.

> >>>*step-by-step*

Missing Sync for BlackBerry

We discussed this application in the Prologue, so you should have it installed already. If not, please take a few minutes to follow the installation instructions for Missing Sync for BlackBerry in the Prologue.

Let's start with music.

1. On the main Missing Sync for BlackBerry screen, check the box next to Music and double-click Music to see the settings.

2. On the Music Settings screen, check the boxes next to the iTunes Playlists that you want on your BlackBerry Curve.

3. You can change the Always maintain at least *X*MB free on storage card, or leave it at the default of 5MB.

4. If you want Missing Sync for BlackBerry to refresh the Smart Playlists (which are the dynamic playlists in iTunes, such as Top 25 Most Played), check this box.

5. Choose when to synchronize your playlists—either on each connection, or by choosing a number of hours between syncs.

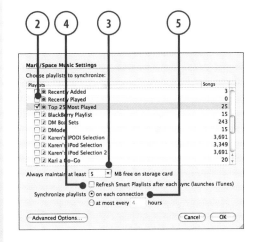

Note

Missing Sync for BlackBerry does not allow you to create new playlists; it can only synchronize existing playlists. If you need to create a new playlist, close Missing Sync for BlackBerry, open iTunes, and create one or more new playlists. Drag the songs you want to those playlists. When you have your playlists ready, run Missing Sync for BlackBerry again, return to this screen, and choose those playlists.

6. Click Advanced Options.

7. On the Advanced screen, you can add extra music file types if your BlackBerry Curve supports them.

8. Click OK.

9. Click OK again to return to the main Missing Sync screen.

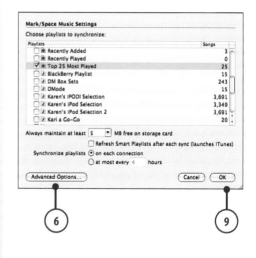

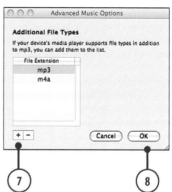

>>>step-by-step

Synchronizing Photos with Missing Sync

Missing Sync for BlackBerry can also synchronize photos with your BlackBerry Curve. This includes importing photos you have taken on your BlackBerry Curve to iPhoto, and exporting photos from iPhoto to your BlackBerry Curve.

1. On the main Missing Sync for BlackBerry screen, check the box next to Photos, and double-click Photos to see the settings.

2. To export photos from iPhoto, check the box next to Export photos to device.

3. You see the iPhoto albums. You can check the ones you want exported to your BlackBerry Curve.

4. For Size, leave it at Full-size images.

5. Choose how often you want the pictures to be exported. By default this is set to on each sync, but you can change it to sync every X hours.

6. Click OK.

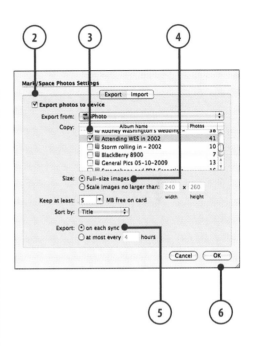

Note

If you do not have a media card in your BlackBerry Curve, you may want to set the Size to Scale images no larger than and set the Photo size to something that is closest to your BlackBerry Curve's screen size. The screen sizes are as follows:

- BlackBerry Curve 8300: 320×240
- BlackBerry Curve 8500: 320×240
- BlackBerry Curve 8900: 480×360

Setting the options this way means that you can fit many more photos on your BlackBerry. Because you are reducing the photos' size to be as close to the BlackBerry Curve's screen size as possible, you can enjoy them on your BlackBerry. But if you send them to someone else (covered later), they may appear quite small on that person's computer screen. This is still a great option for saving space if you have no media card inserted.

7. Click the Import button next to the Export button to have Missing Sync import photos from your BlackBerry Curve.

8. If you want to import photos from your BlackBerry Curve into iPhoto, check the box next to Import photos from device.

9. Select where to download the photos to. By default this would be an album in iPhoto that you created previously. However, it could just be a folder on your Mac, such as the Pictures folder.

10. If you always want to import all photos, even if they have already been imported, check the box next to Import all items, including those previously imported.

11. If you want to remove any photos from your BlackBerry Curve after they have been imported into iPhoto, check the box next to Remove items from device after importing.

12. Click OK.

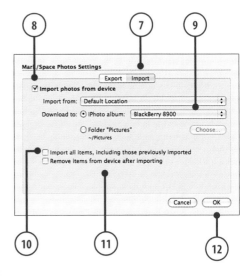

Note

To copy videos to your BlackBerry Curve, simply drag them onto Missing Sync for BlackBerry while it is running. They are automatically converted and prepared for your BlackBerry Curve. If you want to see where your videos go while waiting for the next sync, from the main Missing Sync screen, click the Install button. Your videos are listed there.

>>>step-by-step

Synchronizing Videos with Missing Sync

Missing Sync for BlackBerry can synchronize videos with your BlackBerry Curve. This includes videos you have taken on your BlackBerry Curve being imported to your Mac, and videos on your Mac being converted and exported to your BlackBerry Curve.

1. On the main Missing Sync for BlackBerry screen, check the box next to Video, and double-click Video to see the settings.

2. If you want to import video from your BlackBerry Curve to your Mac, check the box next to Import videos from device.

3. Select where they will be downloaded to. This defaults to an iPhoto album called Photos. You can select a different album.

4. If you always want to import all video, check the box next to Import all videos, including those previously imported.

5. If you want to remove videos from your BlackBerry Curve after they have been imported to your Mac, check the box next to Remove videos from device after importing.

6. Click OK.

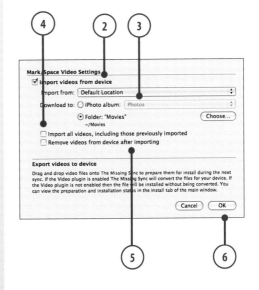

Enjoying Multimedia on Your BlackBerry Curve

Now that you've learned how to get pictures, music, and video onto your BlackBerry Curve, we cover how to take pictures and record movies on the go, as well as play back those great tunes you synchronized earlier.

>>>*step-by-step*

The BlackBerry Curve Camera

All BlackBerry Curve models have cameras. The cameras on the BlackBerry Curve 8300 series and the BlackBerry Curve 8520 are 2-megapixel. The camera on the BlackBerry Curve 8900 is a 3.2-megapixel with autofocus.

With the exception of the BlackBerry Curve 8520, all models have a camera flash.

1. To activate the camera, press the right-side convenience button. By default this button launches the camera.

2. When the camera starts, press the right-side convenience button again to take a picture.

3. When you have previewed the pictures on the screen, press the right-side convenience button again to be ready for your next shot.

The BlackBerry Curve camera can also be used to shoot video.

Note

If you have the BlackBerry Curve 8900, the right-side convenience button has two positions, halfway in and all the way in. If you press the button lightly, it goes in halfway, the camera begins to focus, and you see a white box on the screen. When the camera is in focus, the box turns green. At that point, press the button all the way in, and the camera takes the picture.

4. From the BlackBerry Home Screen, click the Applications folder.

5. In the Applications folder, click the Video Camera icon.

6. To record video, click the trackball or trackpad, and start shooting.

7. To pause recording video, click the trackball or trackpad again.

8. To stop recording, scroll to the stop icon, and click the trackball or trackpad. Your BlackBerry then saves the video.

Note

If you want to use the camera's flash as a video light, before you start recording, press the space-bar. This activates the video light. Record as normal. The surprisingly bright light will illuminate your subjects. To turn off the light, stop recording first, and then press the spacebar again.

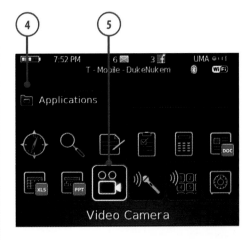

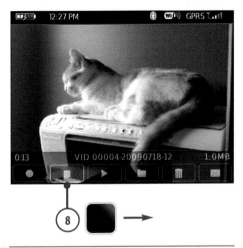

Note

Taking photos with the BlackBerry Curve's camera works very well in bright-light situations, but when you are indoors or in other low-light situations, the pictures can get grainy and blurry.

To combat this, when you are in low-light situations, try to keep your BlackBerry as still as possible when taking the picture. Try to hold you breath, because this helps lessen your body movement. When you press the button to take the picture, try to squeeze the button instead of pressing it. This also helps lessen the BlackBerry's movement.

>>>*step-by-step*

The BlackBerry Curve Media Player

The Media Player is a single built-in BlackBerry application that allows you to play your music and videos and view your photos.

To access the Media Player, click the Media Player icon on the BlackBerry Home Screen.

We now go through all the Media Player's functions. Music is first.

1. To listen to music, click Music.

2. The main Music screen allows you to browse all your music, or browse by Artists, Albums, or Genres.

3. The Sample Songs menu allows you to play any sample songs that were pre-loaded on your BlackBerry Curve.

4. The Shuffle Songs menu plays your music in random order.

5. The Playlists menu shows your playlists.

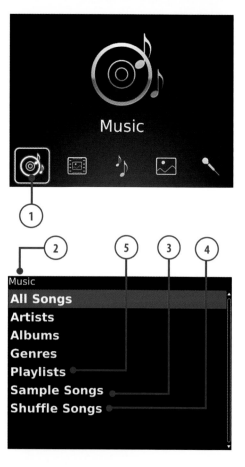

6. To create a new playlist click [New Playlist].

7. You are asked to choose between a Standard Playlist and an Automatic Playlist.

Note

A Standard Playlist is one that you create and manually add songs to. When you create and set up an Automatic Playlist, your BlackBerry watches when you import music and automatically adds to the playlist based on criteria such as artist.

8. Choose Standard Playlist. (To create an Automatic Playlist, go to step 14.)

9. Type a name for your playlist.

10. Click the Menu button, and choose Add Songs.

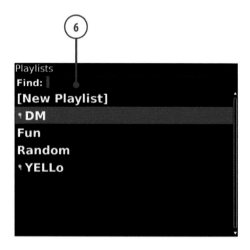

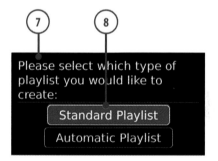

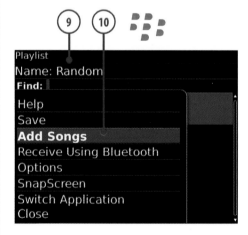

11. If your music list is large, you can start typing the song or artist name, and the list of songs is filtered automatically based on the letters you type.

12. Click a song to add it to your playlist.

13. When all your songs are listed, press the Escape key and choose Save.

14. To create an Automatic Playlist, click New Playlist as before and then choose Automatic Playlist.

Note

Your BlackBerry generates Automatic Playlists based on your choices on this screen. For example, if you wanted this playlist to contain all songs by Depeche Mode, you would click the + next to Artists and choose Depeche Mode. You must already have at least one song by that artist on your BlackBerry in order to do this. After you save the playlist, your BlackBerry automatically creates this playlist for you. It continues to do so when you add new music to your BlackBerry.

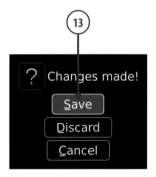

15. Type a name for the playlist.

16. Use the + to the right of each category to add Artists, Albums, or Genres.

Note

While music is playing, you can use other applications on your BlackBerry Curve.

At any time, use the Volume Up/Down button to control the music's volume, no matter which application you are using.

If you receive a phone call while listening to music, your BlackBerry Curve pauses the music. When the call ends, it resumes playing.

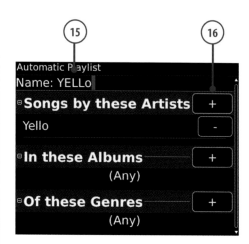

Working with Videos

The BlackBerry Curve Media Player can also play back your videos. These could be videos you have recorded on your BlackBerry Curve, or videos that you have synchronized from your computer.

1. To access Videos, click the Videos icon from the Media Player main screen.

2. To play a video, use the trackball or trackpad to scroll to the video, and click.

3. To record a video, use the trackball or trackpad to scroll up to Video Camera, and click. To learn more about recording video, read "The BlackBerry Curve Camera" section earlier in this chapter.

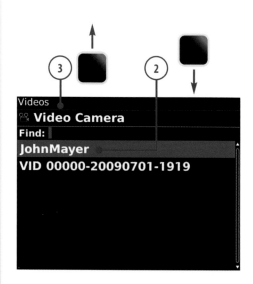

4. To send a video to someone using Bluetooth, press the Menu button and choose Send Using Bluetooth. Some preloaded videos will not send via Bluetooth. A good example is the John Mayer video.

5. While a video is playing, you can skip forward or backward by clicking the trackball or trackpad, scrolling to the progress bar above the play button, clicking the trackball or trackpad again, and scrolling left or right to go backward or forward.

>>>step-by-step

Working with Ring Tones

The Media Player allows you to work with your ring tones. These may be ring tones you have downloaded from websites, or imported from your computer.

1. To access ring tones, click the Ring Tones icon from the Media Player's main screen.

2. Under My Ring Tones, you will find any ring tones that you have received from others or that you created and sent to yourself.

3. To send your ring tones to others via email, MMS, or Bluetooth, press the Menu button, and choose either Send As Email, Send As MMS, or Send Using Bluetooth.

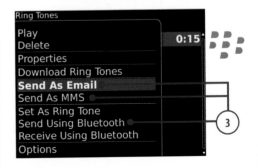

4. Ring tones that are not in the My Ring Tones area are locked and cannot be sent to others.

5. To set any of the ring tones as your current ring tone, press the Menu button and choose Set As Ring Tone.

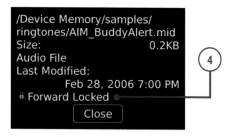

>>>step-by-step

Working with Pictures

The Media Player allows you to work with pictures. These could be pictures that you have taken on your BlackBerry Curve, or pictures that you have exported from your computer.

1. To access Pictures, click the Pictures icon from the Media Players main screen.

2. To take a picture, use the trackball or trackpad to scroll up to Camera, and click.

3. To view the pictures on your BlackBerry Curve, click All Pictures. They appear in a grid pattern.

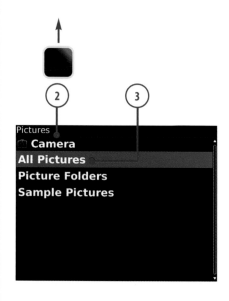

4. To view one of the pictures, click it.

5. To zoom in on a picture, while it is open click the trackball or track-pad and choose Zoom.

6. The Zoom slider appears on the top left of the picture. Scroll up or down with the trackball or track-pad to zoom in and out.

7. To rotate the picture, click the trackball or trackpad, and choose Rotate.

8. To set a picture as your BlackBerry Curve's Home Screen image, click the trackball or trackpad, and choose Set As Home Screen Image.

9. To reset your Home Screen image to the theme default, choose Reset Home Screen Image.

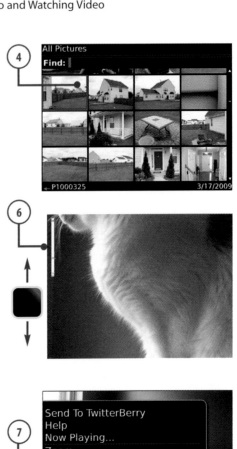

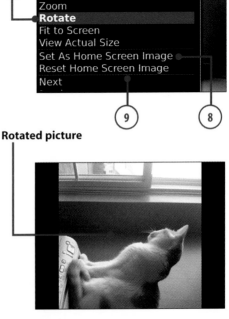

Rotated picture

10. To send the picture to someone or a computer using Bluetooth, click the trackball or trackpad, and choose Send Using Bluetooth.

11. Select the Bluetooth device that you previously associated your BlackBerry with.

12. The picture is sent.

13. To send someone the picture by email, click the Menu button, and choose Send As Email.

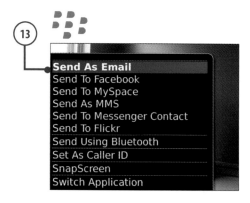

14. A new email opens on the BlackBerry Curve's screen with the picture attached. Choose a recipient, and send.

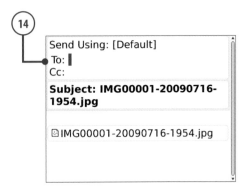

>>>*step-by-step*

Working with Voice Notes

Media Player allows you to work with your voice notes. Voice notes are the electronic equivalent of the old dictaphones that used small cassette tapes.

1. To access voice notes, click the Voice Notes icon from the Media Player's main screen.

2. To record a voice note, use the trackball or trackpad to scroll up to Record, and click.

3. Click the trackball or trackpad to start recording the voice note.

4. To listen to a voice note, click it.

5. To send a voice note to someone via email, MMS, BlackBerry messenger, or Bluetooth, scroll to the voice note, click the Menu button, and choose the appropriate menu option.

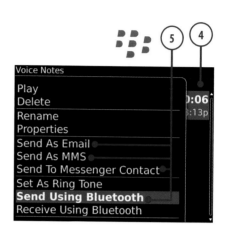

Configuring the Media Player

The Media Player can be configured to work the way you like, so let's explore how to do that.

1. To configure the Media Player, from any Media Player screen, click the Menu button and choose Options.

2. Under General is Device Memory Limit, set to 15MB. This setting limits the amount of memory used in the BlackBerry Curve's main memory for pictures. If you have a media card inserted, you can lower this value to 5MB, which gives your applications more space to use. If you do not have a media card inserted, all multimedia you load is stored in your BlackBerry's main memory. You should leave this at 15MB.

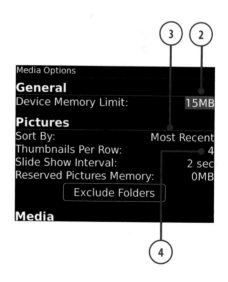

3. Under Pictures, the first setting is Sort By. This can be set to Most Recent or Name.

4. Next is Thumbnails Per Row. This is set to 4, but you can change it from 3 all the way up to 8.

5. Next is Slide Show Interval. It is set to 2 seconds, but you can change it from 1 second all the way up to 15 seconds.

6. Next is Reserved Pictures Memory. This can be set to 0 to 2MB. This setting is really irrelevant, though, because it is overridden by the Device Memory Limit.

7. Next is a button called Exclude Folders. If you click it, you can choose which folders on your media card must be excluded when using the Media Player. This can be useful if you use applications that store their own multimedia on the media card, and you don't want them showing up in your list of available multimedia.

8. Under Media, the first option is Turn Off Auto Backlighting. It is set to Yes. Setting it to Yes tells your BlackBerry Curve to disable the normal automatic backlighting mechanism when playing media such as videos. If you set this to No, your BlackBerry continues to use its automatic backlighting mechanism while you play media, which may reduce battery life.

9. Next is Audio Boost. Turning this on makes any media you are playing extra loud.

10. Next is Headset Equalizer. By default this is set to Off. But if you click, you can set the equalizer to a multitude of options that will enhance audio when played through a headset (Bluetooth or cable attached).

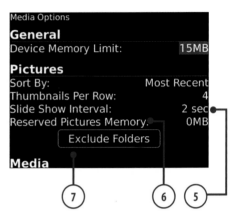

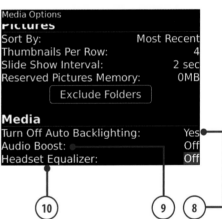

Bluetooth indicator

Web browser

In this chapter, you learn about connecting. This includes connecting to devices and networks. Topics include the following:

→ Connecting to the Internet using Wi-Fi
→ Connecting using virtual private networks (VPNs)
→ Connecting via Bluetooth

4

Connecting: Internet, Bluetooth, and VPNs

The BlackBerry Curve can connect to the Internet via the cellular network or Wi-Fi. It can also connect to networks via virtual private networks (VPNs) for secure communications. Finally, it can connect to devices such as headsets and computers via Bluetooth.

Connecting your BlackBerry to the Internet has the benefit of allowing you to browse the Web, as well as use applications that need Internet access. Bluetooth devices can range from headsets, to other phones, to computers. Connecting to these devices allows you to talk on the phone using hands-free headsets, and exchange information with others while connected to their phones or computers.

Finally, VPNs can be useful for getting access to closed networks like a company's intranet.

Connecting to the Internet

Your BlackBerry Curve would not be a smartphone if it did not allow you to connect to the Internet and browse the Web. Without your doing anything, the BlackBerry Curve uses the cellular network to connect to the Internet. This connection is not terribly fast, but it is acceptable. The BlackBerry Curve uses a General Packet Radio Service (GPRS), Enhanced Data Rates for GSM Evolution (EDGE), or Evolution Data Optimized (EVDO) cellular network to connect so all BlackBerry applications and the web browser can connect automatically.

>>>*step-by-step*

Connecting to the Internet Via Wi-Fi

If you are in range of a Wi-Fi network, such as at home, a coffee shop, an airport lounge, or a client's office, you can make use of the extra speed boost by connecting your BlackBerry to that network if your BlackBerry supports it.

Do the following to connect to a Wi-Fi hot spot:

1. From the BlackBerry Home Screen, select the Settings folder.

2. From the Settings folder, select Set Up Wi-Fi.

3. On the Set Up Wi-Fi Connection main screen, click Scan For Networks.

4. Your BlackBerry scans the area for wireless networks in range.

5. After a short while, you see a list of wireless networks in range. Each network is listed by name, and a signal meter shows the signal strength. Under the name of the wireless network you see the type of encryption being used, such as WPA2-Personal or WEP. The padlock icon indicates that the wireless network is encrypted and not open.

6. If the wireless network is closed or using encryption, you are prompted to enter an encryption key. You need to find out what this key is ahead of time.

7. Click Connect. Your BlackBerry displays a screen indicating that it is connecting to the wireless network.

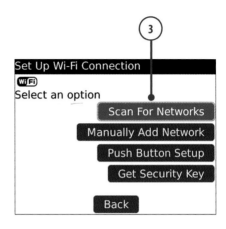

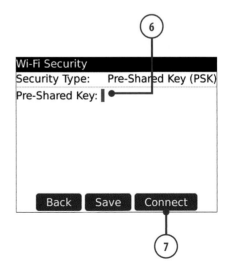

8. If your BlackBerry Curve can connect, you see the Connection Successful! screen. This screen also shows the name of the wireless network. You can change this name to something like Home or Work, or leave it as is and click Next.

9. If you have a previously configured VPN profile, you are prompted with the VPN Selection screen. If you do not want to use a VPN connection over this Wi-Fi network, change Use VPN with this Wi-Fi Profile? to No.

10. Click Next.

11. On the final Wi-Fi setup screen, if you know ahead of time that the Wi-Fi network you just connected to will require further login via a web page, click Wi-Fi Hotspot Login. These kinds of networks typically are at hotels or airport lounges.

Wi-Fi Hotspot Login

If you need to take the final step of completing your connection to the Wi-Fi Hotspot by logging into a web page, when you click Wi-Fi Hotspot Login, the web browser loads and takes you straight to the login page. There you need to provide a username or password, a credit card, or your room number depending on where you are. Once you have provided the relevant information, you are taken back to this final screen.

12. Click Finish.

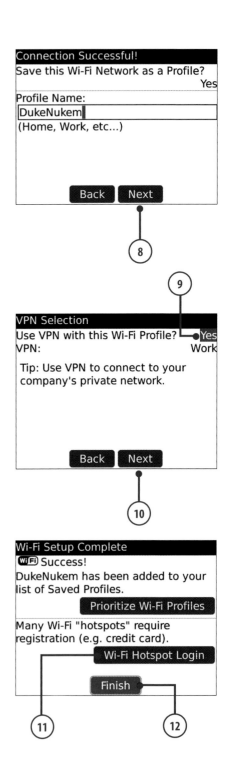

Connecting to an Invisible Wi-Fi Network

If the wireless network you want to connect to is not broadcasting its name or SSID, you can manually set up a connection to this network.

1. From the Set Up Wi-Fi Connection main screen, click Manually Add Network.

2. Type in the wireless network name or SSID and click Add.

3. Select the type of security used by the wireless network.

4. If you have to use some kind of security, type in the relevant details such as the key or username and password, then click Connect.

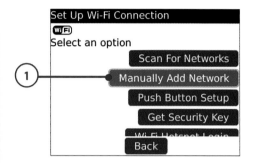

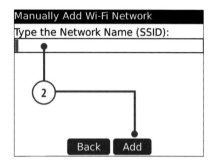

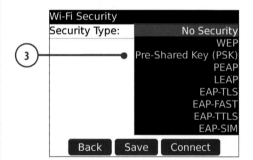

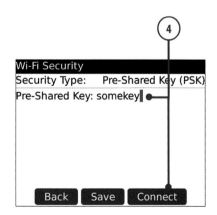

5. If you entered the details correctly, you see the Connection Successful! screen. Click Next.

6. If you have a previously configured VPN profile, you are prompted with the VPN Selection screen. If you do not want to use a VPN connection over this Wi-Fi network, change Use VPN with this Wi-Fi Profile? to No, and click Next.

7. On the final Wi-Fi setup screen, you can click Finish. If you know ahead of time that the Wi-Fi network you just connected to requires further login via a web page, click Wi-Fi Hotspot Login. These kinds of networks typically are at hotels or airport lounges.

8. Click Finish.

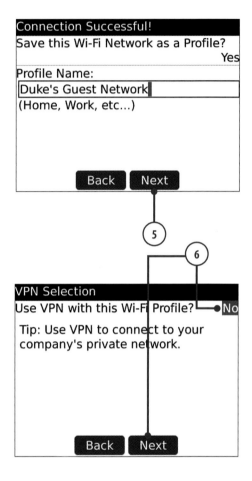

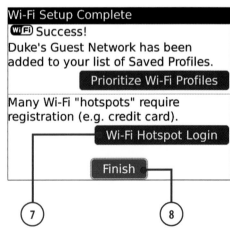

>>>*step-by-step*

Diagnosing Wi-Fi Network Issues

If you need to edit or diagnose your Wi-Fi connections later, you can do so by running Manage Connections.

1. From the BlackBerry Home Screen, click Manage Connections.

2. On the next screen, select Wi-Fi Options.

3. The Wi-Fi Connections screen shows all configured Wi-Fi networks. This list includes the network you are currently connected to, as well as wireless networks you previously set up and have connected to in the past.

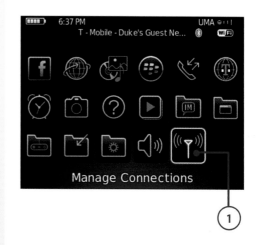

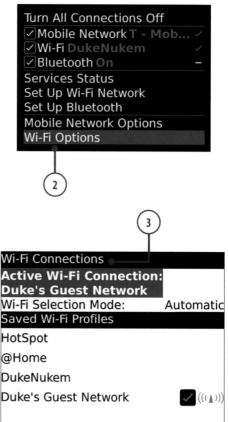

4. If you need to diagnose a wireless network issue, click the Menu key, and choose Wi-Fi Tools.

5. To run Wi-Fi diagnostics, choose Wi-Fi Diagnostics.

6. Change the diagnostic mode to Advanced by pressing the Menu button and choosing Options.

7. Change the Display Mode to Advanced.

8. To save your settings, press the Menu key, and choose Save. Pressing the Escape key here does not save the settings, as it does in other BlackBerry screens.

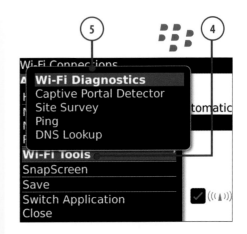

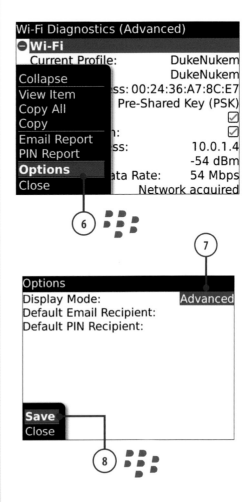

9. The advanced Wi-Fi Diagnostics screen appears. This screen lists diagnostics for Wi-Fi, VPN connections (if any), UMA connection, and connection to the RIM NOC.

10. If you choose Site Survey from the Wi-Fi Tools menu, you can run a Wi-Fi site survey, which helps determine wireless interference. To start the scan, press the Menu key, and choose Start Scan.

11. The scan displays all the wireless networks in range, along with technical information about each one.

12. If you need to send the site survey results to someone for support purposes, press the Menu key, and choose Send As E-mail or Send As Pin.

Auto Connecting to Wi-Fi

When you have one or more Wi-Fi networks set up on your BlackBerry Curve, anytime you are within range of those networks, your BlackBerry automatically connects to them, giving you the extra speed benefit and, if your carrier supports UMA, the benefit of free calling.

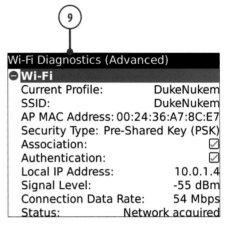

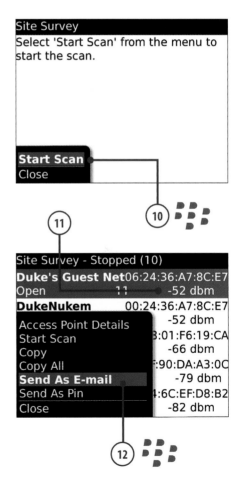

Virtual Private Networks (VPNs)

Typically, if you have a corporate BlackBerry, you do not need to use a VPN to connect to your company's intranet. This is because your BlackBerry already provides a secure connection to your company's intranet via the BlackBerry Enterprise Server. However, if for some reason your company requires this, or you are using a personal BlackBerry and you need to access one of your client's intranets, you may be asked to use a VPN.

>>>*step-by-step*

Creating a VPN

Follow these steps to set up a VPN:

1. Click Settings from the BlackBerry Home Screen.

2. From the Settings Folder, click Options.

3. From the Options screen, click Security Options.

4. From the Security Options screen, click VPN.

5. To add a new VPN Profile, press the Menu key, and choose New. The VPN settings are supplied to you, so from here you need to make selections and enter the supplied information.

6. After you select New, you are asked to choose the VPN Vendor.

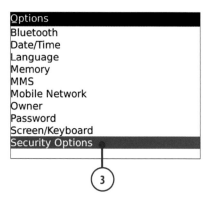

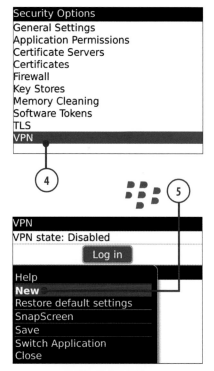

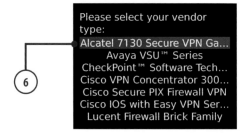

7. After you make that selection, you see the main VPN Profile screen. Enter all the information provided to you on this screen.

8. As soon as everything has been entered, press the Escape key, and choose Save.

```
VPN Profile
Name: Work
Gateway type:
            Cisco Secure PIX Firewall VPN
Concentrator address:
Group name:
Group password:
User name:
User password:
■Save passphrase
■Dynamically determine DNS
IP address:
```

```
VPN Profile
■Dynamically determine DNS
IP address:
Subnet mask:
Primary DNS:
Secondary DNS:
Domain name:
■Enable extended authentication
IKE DH group:              Group 1
IKE cipher:          DES (56-bit key)
IKE hash:       HMAC MD5 (128-bits)
□Perfect Forward Secrecy
```

```
VPN Profile
IKE DH group:              Group 1
IKE cipher:          DES (56-bit key)
IKE hash:       HMAC MD5 (128-bits)
■Perfect Forward Secrecy
IPSec crypto and hash suite:
                        NONE-MD5
NAT timeout (in minutes): 1
■Use hard token
Software Token Serial Number:
                  <None available>
□Disable VPN banner
```

Connecting Via Bluetooth

Your BlackBerry Curve has a built-in Bluetooth radio that can be used to connect to other phones, accessories, and computers.

When it is connected to other phones or computers, you can transfer files and contacts. If you connect your BlackBerry to your car's Bluetooth, different levels of integration can happen, such as hands-free dialing and contact synchronization.

>>>*step-by-step*

Pairing Your BlackBerry

Follow these steps to pair your BlackBerry with another phone, Bluetooth accessory, or computer:

1. Click Settings on the BlackBerry Home Screen.

2. Click Set Up Bluetooth from the Settings folder.

3. Click Search to find available Bluetooth devices.

    After your BlackBerry scans the area, it lists the Bluetooth devices it has discovered.

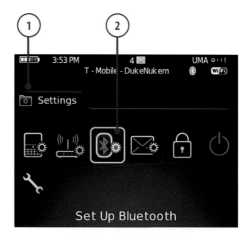

4. To pair with a device, use the trackball or trackpad to click that device.

5. Your BlackBerry asks you to type in a numeric code. The same code you enter on your BlackBerry must be entered on the phone or computer you are pairing with. After you both enter the same code, your devices are paired.

   Some phones or computers require that you put them in Listen Mode so that they can be discovered. Make sure you do this before attempting to pair with them.

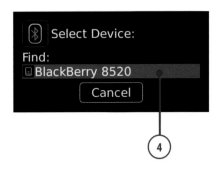

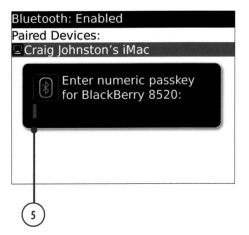

Note

If you are pairing with a Bluetooth accessory such as a wireless Bluetooth headset, you need to find out the predetermined code that must be used to pair with it. Because there is no way to type a number on your headset, the headset always uses the same code. This code is almost always 0000. When pairing with a headset, put the headset into Listen Mode as per the manufacturer's instructions. When your BlackBerry finds the headset and asks you to enter the numeric code, enter 0000.

6. After you have paired with a phone, accessory, or computer, click that device, and choose Device Properties.

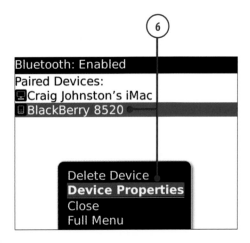

7. Device Name is automatically populated from the device you paired with, but you may want to rename it. Many headsets simply list the model number as their name, so you would probably want to rename it to headset.

8. Trusted shows whether you trust the device. It defaults to Prompt. You can change it to Yes or No. It is recommended that you select Yes if you trust the device or if it is your computer. If you do not trust it, each time you connect, you are prompted.

9. Encryption allows you to set whether to encrypt the data that goes back and forth between your BlackBerry Curve and the device you paired with. It is a good idea to leave it set to Enabled in case someone is trying to listen in or capture packets of data over the air.

10. The Services are the available services that the device you paired with offers.

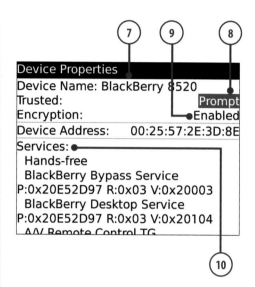

>>>*step-by-step*

Bluetooth Options

You may want to change how your BlackBerry supports Bluetooth. For example, you may want to change the name by which your BlackBerry advertises itself, or make your BlackBerry undiscoverable.

1. To change your Bluetooth options, from the Bluetooth main screen, press the Menu button, and choose Options.

2. Device Name is the name by which your BlackBerry advertises itself. It defaults to the name of your BlackBerry, such as BlackBerry 8900. You can change it to something like Craig's BlackBerry.

3. Discoverable is where you set whether your BlackBerry is discoverable. If you set this to Yes, your BlackBerry is always discoverable if someone else is doing a Bluetooth search.

4. Allow Outgoing Calls controls whether someone or something can use your BlackBerry to make outgoing phone calls. It is best to leave this set to Never unless you use your BlackBerry to make outgoing calls from another device.

5. Contacts Transfer allows you to control whether someone or something can request a transfer of your Contacts. If you set this to Disables, this cannot happen. You can set this to All Entries, Hotlist Only, or Selected Categories Only.

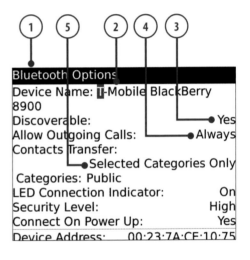

2-Minute Rule

If you set this to 2 minutes, your BlackBerry is discoverable for only 2 minutes, and then it changes this setting to No.

Setting this to 2 Minutes is useful if you want someone to be able to find your BlackBerry Curve right away, but then you want your BlackBerry to become invisible again.

After you have paired with a device, you no longer need to leave your device in discoverable mode.

6. LED Connection Indicator allows you to set whether the blue LED flashes when you are communicating with a Bluetooth device.

7. Security Level controls the Bluetooth security. It can be set to High or High+Encryption.

8. Connect On Power Up allows you to set whether the Bluetooth radio is enabled when you power up your BlackBerry Curve.

9. Under Services, you can enable or disable which Bluetooth services you want to make available by checking or unchecking the boxes.

10. Press the Escape key, and choose Save to save your changes.

Contact Categories

If you choose Selected Categories Only, you can scroll down to the next line, click the Menu button, and choose Categories.

If you have a vehicle that has Bluetooth, you may need to allow Contacts Transfer. Many Bluetooth-enabled vehicles transfer the contacts to memory in the vehicle to make dialing from the vehicle's onboard systems easier.

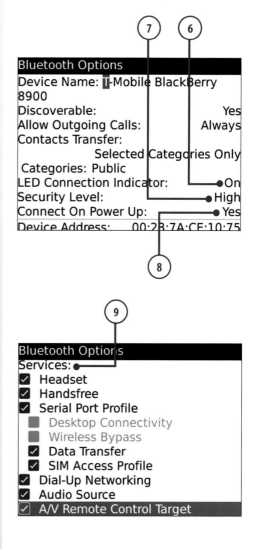

New email indicator

Email

In this chapter, you learn about email on your BlackBerry Curve. Topics include the following:

→ Configuring corporate and personal email
→ Configuring email settings
→ Managing email accounts
→ Working with email
→ Typing tips

5

Email

Email is what made the BlackBerry famous. Email is what it was originally built for, and it still excels at it.

The BlackBerry supports push email, which means that it does not poll for emails on a schedule, but rather the BlackBerry server pushes the emails out to the BlackBerry when it receives them.

If you have a corporate BlackBerry, the BlackBerry Enterprise Server (BES) receives emails instantly in real time as soon as they arrive in your Inbox. The BES then pushes those emails out to your BlackBerry in real time.

If you have a personal BlackBerry, your wireless carrier utilizes a version of the BlackBerry server called the BlackBerry Internet Server (BIS). Like the BES, the BIS pushes emails out to your BlackBerry in real time as soon as it receives them; however, the BIS does not necessarily receive emails from your personal email account instantly in real time.

If you have Gmail, Yahoo Mail, or the wireless carrier-supplied BlackBerry email account yourname@carrier.blackberry.net, BIS should receive those emails in real time and send them to your BlackBerry in real time.

If you have other mail services, the BIS polls for email. When you set up email on your BlackBerry for the first time, BIS checks for email. It then waits 15 minutes and checks again. If it does not find email, it waits another 15 minutes to check. If it does find email, it collects it and pushes it to your BlackBerry. BIS then switches to a 3-minute polling cycle. If it does not find email after five polls at 3-minute intervals, it switches back to a 15-minute poll cycle.

Regardless of how the BES and BIS get the email for you, the push technology is what enables a BlackBerry to have such great battery life. Because the BlackBerry is not polling for emails, it is not using up battery power. This enables the BlackBerry to always outlast other smartphones.

Configuring Email Accounts

You can set up two types of email accounts on your BlackBerry.

The first is a personal email account, which you set up on a BIS. The BIS enables you to have up to 10 personal email accounts on your BlackBerry.

The second type of account is a corporate email account. You can have only one corporate email account on your BlackBerry Curve. If you have a corporate BlackBerry, your company might block personal email accounts. If it doesn't block personal email, your BlackBerry can have both corporate and personal email on it at the same time.

Setting Up Personal Email Accounts

Personal email accounts can be on any on-line email service that allows remote connections using POP3 or IMAP. Sometimes you have to enable these features before attempting to set up your BlackBerry for personal email.

1. From your BlackBerry Home Screen, click the Settings icon.

2. From the Settings folder, click Manage Internet Email. You will be asked to add an existing email account to your BlackBerry.

Wireless Coverage Required

Clicking this icon takes you to a special mobile website hosted by your wireless carrier. This mobile website enables you to set up one or more email accounts on your BlackBerry. Because of this you need to be in wireless coverage to complete these steps.

3. Enter your existing email address and password. Click Next. The website sets up your account based on this information if the email account is with a well-known email service like Gmail or Yahoo.

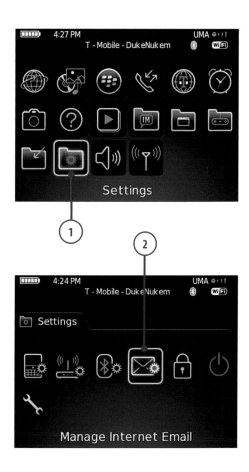

4. If your email account is known by the BlackBerry servers, you see a success screen telling you that your account is now set up on your BlackBerry.

5. If your email account is not with a recognized service, choose the option that says I will provide the settings to add this email account and click Next.

6. Choose whether this email account is an Internet Service Provider Email (POP/IMAP) or small business email account that can be accessed via Outlook Web Access (OWA).

7. If this is a personal BlackBerry, you likely need to select Internet Service Provider Email.

Set Up Your Mailbox First

Some email services require that you first enable access to your mailbox via POP or IMAP before you run through the setup on your BlackBerry. Check with your email service provider first and enable the correct settings before proceeding.

8. On the next screen, provide your account username and password. The username is often just your full email address. You also need to provide your email server address. Click Next.

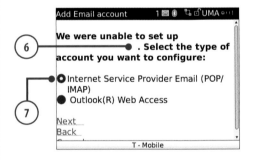

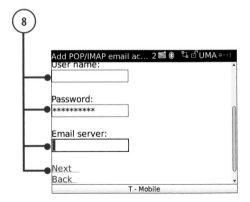

POP3 or IMAP

If at all possible, always use IMAP as a method to access your mailbox. IMAP is a newer technology that enables more integration with your mailbox and has extra features such as marking an email read on your mailbox when you read it on your BlackBerry. POP (which is short for POP3) is a much older technology, and although it still works, there is no mailbox integration.

9. If you entered all the information correctly, the next screen shows that you have successfully set up your email.

10. On your BlackBerry you receive an email from the activation server telling you that you will begin receiving emails from that email account in approximately 20 minutes.

11. You can have up to 10 personal email accounts on your BlackBerry. If you need to add more personal email accounts, start at step 2 again.

How to Determine Your Mail Server

This is typically imap.*<your domain name>.<domain extension>*. For example, if your email address were craig@ussenterprise.gov, the mail server would be imap.ussenterprise. gov or pop.ussenterprise.gov. You can always find out the exact mail server names by contacting your email service provider.

>>>*step-by-step*

Setting Up a Corporate Email Account

If you have a corporate BlackBerry, before you set up an email account, your BlackBerry administrator needs to add you to one of your company's BlackBerry Enterprise servers and provide you with an Enterprise activation password. You can then continue with the following steps:

1. From the BlackBerry Home Screen, click the Setting icon.

2. From within the Setting folder, click the Setup Wizard icon.

3. After the Setup Wizard loads, click Email Setup.

4. Select I want to use a work email account with a BlackBerry Enterprise Server and click Next.

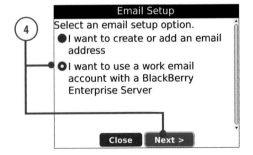

5. On the next screen, select Yes and
    click Next.

Enterprise Activation
Password

Your administrator must provide
you with your Enterprise
Activation password before you
can continue.

6. On the Enterprise Activation
    screen, enter your corporate email
    address.

7. Enter the Enterprise Activation
    password that your BlackBerry
    Administrator gave you.

8. Unless instructed by your
    BlackBerry administrator, leave
    the Activation Server Address
    field blank.

9. Press the trackball or trackpad
    and choose Activate.

Your BlackBerry now begins the
Enterprise Activation process.
Depending on your company's
BlackBerry setup, your BlackBerry is
set up for wireless email, calendar,
tasks, MemoPad (Notes), and corporate web browsing.

You see a screen that says Activation
Complete after your BlackBerry is
fully activated.

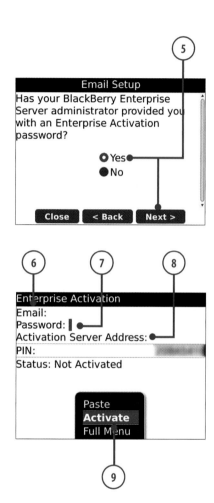

Working with Email

Now that you have your email accounts set up, you can send and receive email and depending on whether you have a corporate email account or personal email account, you can delete email, move email to folders, and flag emails for follow-up.

>>>*step-by-step*

Composing Email

1. From the BlackBerry Home Screen, click the Messages icon. If you are on the BlackBerry Today screen, you also see the Messages icon.

What Is in Messages?

The Messages application holds all types of messages including corporate and personal email, BlackBerry PIN messages, SMSs, MMSs, call logs, and Instant Messaging (IM) messages.

2. Click the Menu button and choose Compose Email.

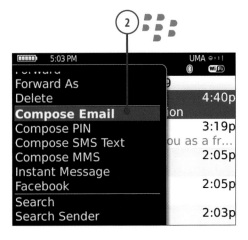

3. Start typing the name of the person you want to send your email to. You can start typing his first or last name (surname). As you type the name, the BlackBerry drops down a list of possible matches.

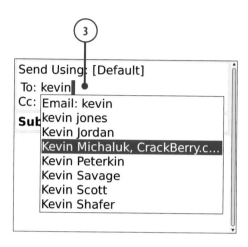

Looking Someone Up

If you have a corporate BlackBerry, as you type in the first or last name of the person you are looking for, you see an extra line with the word Lookup on it. This is for searching your corporate address book. If you want to address the email to someone at your company and his or her name is not in your local address book, click Lookup. The BlackBerry searches your corporate address book for people or groups matching the part of the name you typed in. This search is normally quick, returning a result in a split-second. From the search results, select the name to address the email.

You can repeat these steps to add multiple recipients to the To and CC fields.

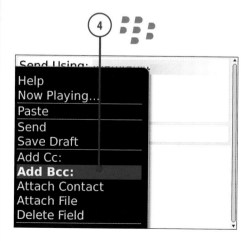

4. If you want to add a blind carbon copy (BCC), click the Menu button and choose Add Bcc. A Bcc field will be added and you can add recipients to that field.

You Don't Need to Type the @ Sign

The BlackBerry Curve has contextual awareness. If you type text into a field that is set for email addresses, you don't actually need to type the @ sign or the dot. The BlackBerry already knows that an email cannot contain spaces, so it uses that information to apply logic to the email field. If you need to type in the email address *someone*@gmail.com, you can actually type *someone* <space> gmail <space> com. The BlackBerry knows that the first space you type needs to be the @ sign and any subsequent spaces need to be periods.

If the email address has periods before the @ sign however, you need to actually type those.

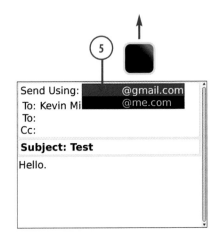

5. If you have more than one email account on your BlackBerry, you can change the account that this email is sent from by scrolling up to the top of the screen and clicking Send Using.

6. After you address your email, type in a subject for the email in the Subject line.

7. To type your email, scroll down to the area under the Subject field and start typing.

8. To change the importance of an email by marking it Low, Normal, or High, click the Menu button and choose Options.

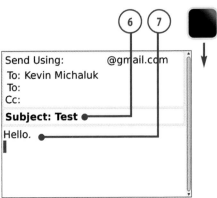

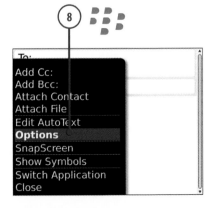

9. Click the Importance field and make your choice of Importance.

10. Press the Escape key and choose Save to save the change.

11. If you are busy typing an email and need to save it and come back to it later, you can save it as a Draft. Press the Escape key and choose Save.

12. This saves your message as a Draft message. You see Draft messages listed in the message list with a green icon with a small pen. If you click on a Draft message, you can continue composing the message and send it normally.

13. If you need to attach someone's contact information from your Address Book, while composing an email, click the Menu button and choose Attach Contact.

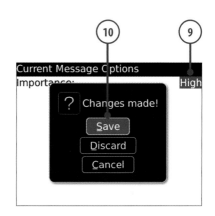

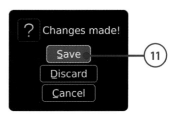

Sending Icon

When you send a message, you see the message list with your message at the top. The message has a Sending icon. Depending on the version of firmware running on your BlackBerry, the icon can be slightly different.

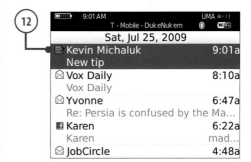

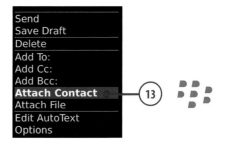

14. Scroll through your address book or start typing the person's first or last name to quickly filter the display. When you find the contact you need to attach, click that contact. The contact's vCard attaches to your email.

15. If you want to attach files stored on your BlackBerry or on your BlackBerry's media card, click the Menu button and choose Attach File.

16. You see a view of your files and folders stored on your BlackBerry and your BlackBerry's media card. Browse the folders to find the file you want to attach and click it.

Red X

If there is a problem sending your message, the icon changes to a red X. Problems sending emails are rare on a BlackBerry, but if you see the red X, scroll to the message, press the Menu key, and choose Resend.

Delete Before Sending

If you have sent a message and it is still sending or waiting to be sent, you can cancel it by scrolling to the message, pressing the Menu key, and choosing Delete.

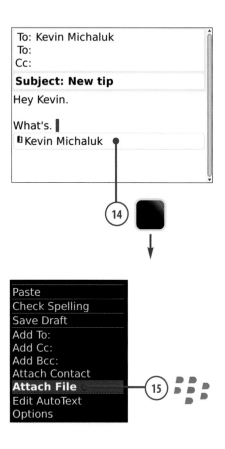

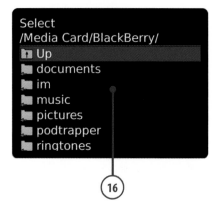

You see your attachments listed at the bottom of your email.

17. After you type in your email, click the trackball or trackpad and choose Send.

Out of Coverage

If you are out of coverage when you send your message, your BlackBerry shows the Waiting icon. When you return to coverage, that message will be sent without any further action from you.

>>>*step-by-step*

AutoText and Other Typing Tips

While typing an email, you can use many shortcuts and tricks to speed up the process.

1. To add a period and a space quickly, press the spacebar twice.

2. If you need to make a character that is not after a period or at the beginning of a new line an uppercase letter, press and hold that key for one-half a second. Your BlackBerry switches it to an uppercase letter.

3. If you type *teh* on your BlackBerry, as you press space, the BlackBerry changes it to *the*. This works with many other words, for example, *acn* becomes *can*, *agian* becomes *again*, *alot* becomes *a lot*, and so on.

To: Kevin Savage
Cc:

Subject: Attachments

Here are some attachments.
|
Craig.

✉ IMG00004-20090716-2122.jpg
📧 VID 00000-20090716-2127.3GP
🔊 VN00001-20090716-2013.amr

Attachments

③

To: Kevin Michaluk
To:
Cc:
Bcc:

Subject: Next podcast

Hi Kevin.

What time should we record teh|
next podcast?

Thanks

③

To: Kevin Michaluk
To:
Cc:
Bcc:

Subject: Next podcast

Hi Kevin.

What time should we record the |
next podcast?

Thanks

4. If you type *il* on your BlackBerry, as you press space, the BlackBerry changes it to *I'll*.

5. To get your BlackBerry to type its phone number, type **mynumber** and press space. The BlackBerry replaces the word mynumber with your actual phone number.

6. To get your BlackBerry to type its PIN, type **mypin** and press space. The BlackBerry replaces the word mypin with your PIN.

Note

Some other useful shortcut words follow:

- **cmd** becomes command
- **hr** becomes hour
- **mn** becomes minute
- **visavis** becomes Vis-à-vis
- **lt** becomes the time
- **ld** becomes the date

To: Kevin Michaluk
To:
Cc:
Bcc:

Subject: Next podcast

Hi Kevin.

What time should we record the next podcast?

||

④

To: Kevin Michaluk
To:
Cc:
Bcc:

Subject: Next podcast

Hi Kevin.

What time should we record the next podcast?

I'll |

④

AutoText

AutoText is powerful and you can use it to your benefit by creating your own AutoText phrases. For example, you can create an AutoText phrase of zzzz to type out quite a lengthy email, or you can add new AutoText phrases that are specific to your industry. To access AutoText, follow these steps:

1. From your BlackBerry Home Screen, click the Settings icon.

2. From within the Settings folder, click Options.

3. When in Options, click AutoText. You see all the built-in AutoText phrases.

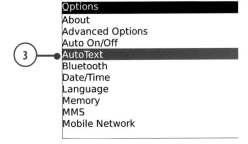

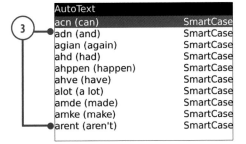

4. To add your own AutoText, click the Menu button and choose New.

5. On the New screen, type in some text that will be replaced with other text. For example, have AutoText replace the text zzzz with Thank you for your time today.

6. We can take this a lot further. Let's really get AutoText working for you. Let's say you are a salesperson and want to send a quick thank you email after each meeting while you are in the elevator. In the Replace field, type **meetleave**.

7. In the With field, type "Thank you for your time today. I enjoyed our meeting and will follow up with you shortly. Please feel free to call or email with any questions or concerns you may have."

8. Press the Escape key and choose Save to save your new AutoText. Now return to the Messages application so that you can test your new AutoText.

9. Compose a new email, address it, enter a subject, and scroll into the body of the email.

10. Type an initial greeting, press enter and type **meetleave**.

11. When you press the spacebar, the word meetleave will be replaced with all the text you entered into the AutoText earlier.

This use of AutoText can greatly cut down on the time it takes to send these kinds of emails.

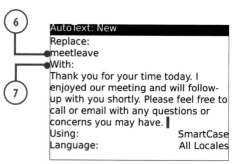

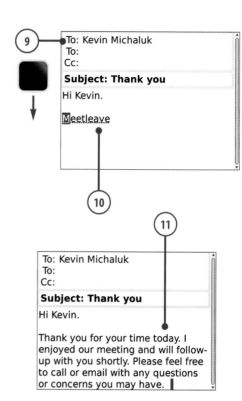

>>>*step-by-step*

Symbols and Accented Characters

While typing an email, you might want to enter an accented or special character.

1. To enter an accented character, such as á, hold down the letter and scroll the trackball or track-pad left or right until you see the accented character you want; then release the letter.

2. To enter a symbol that is not rep-resented on the keyboard, press the Symbol button.

3. Under each symbol is a letter on the keyboard. Press the corre-sponding letter to type the sym-bol. For example, to type the symbol [, type Q.

4. To switch between the symbol screens, press the Symbol button.

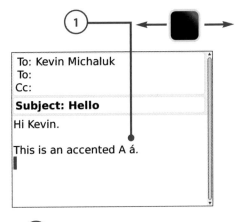

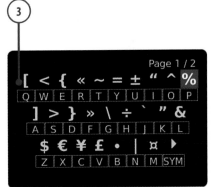

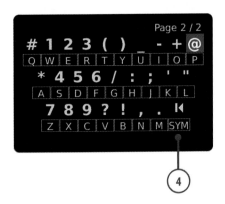

5. If you need to type a word in all CAPS, press the Alt and right-side Shift keys together. This engages Caps lock. When you finish typing the CAPS letters, press the Shift key to disengage Caps lock.

6. If you need to type a series of numbers, you can engage Num Lock by pressing the Alt and left-side Shift keys together. When you finish typing the series of numbers, press the Shift key to disengage Num lock.

>>>*step-by-step*

Copy and Paste

If you need to copy some text and move it somewhere else in your email, you can do this in two ways. The first way is to select text line by line:

1. Hold the Shift key and scroll over the text you need to copy with the trackball or trackpad.

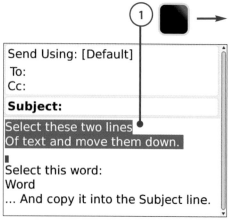

Send Using: [Default]
To:
Cc:

Subject:

Select these two lines
Of text and move them down.

Select this word:
Word
... And copy it into the Subject line.

2. If you need to be more precise and only select text letter by letter, hold the Alt key down and scroll over the text you need to copy with the trackball or trackpad.

3. After you select the text, click the trackball or trackpad and choose Copy.

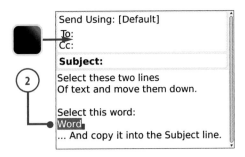

Copy Shortcut

An even quicker way to choose Copy is to hold the Alt key and click the trackball or trackpad.

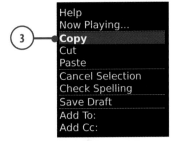

4. To paste the selected text somewhere else in your email, scroll to the location where you need to paste it, press the Menu button, and choose Paste.

Paste Shortcut

An even quicker way to choose Paste is to hold the Shift key and click the trackball or trackpad.

Delete Original Text

If while replying, you want to delete the original text of the email, press the Menu button, and choose Delete Original Text.

Spell Checking Email

The BlackBerry Curve has a built-in
spell checker that you can use to
make sure your emails are error-free.

1. As you type an email, if your
   BlackBerry sees a word that
   it thinks is misspelled, it underlines it.

2. If you scroll over the underlined
   word and click the trackball or
   trackpad, your BlackBerry sug-
   gests corrections to the word. To
   select the correctly spelled word,
   scroll to the correct word and
   click on it.

3. If the word is spelled correctly,
   you can click the Menu button
   and choose to either ignore the
   word or add it to your dictionary.

Receiving and Reading Email

It seems like this is something that
would be self-explanatory; however,
there are a few things that you may
not know about receiving email on a
BlackBerry Curve.

1. When you receive emails on your
   BlackBerry Curve, you receive the
   first two kilobytes (2K) of the
   email. If the email is longer than
   2K, at the bottom of the email,
   you will see a blue line that says
   More Available and the size of the
   rest of the email.

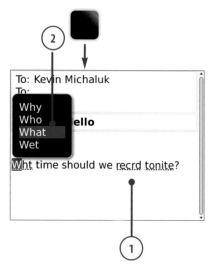

What If You Are Out of Coverage?

If you are out of coverage at the time, you cannot read the next 2K of that email. When you return to coverage, the BlackBerry automatically downloads the next 2K for you and marks the message as unread again.

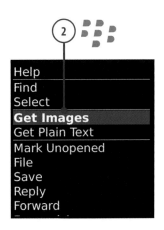

2. Your BlackBerry Curve also supports Rich Text Format (RTF) and HyperText Markup Language (HTML) formatted emails. When you receive one of these emails, you can see all the text formatting that was included in the original email. To load all the images, click the Menu button, and choose Get Images.

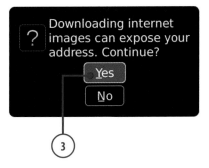

3. You will see a warning that downloading Internet images can expose your address. Click Yes. The BlackBerry then downloads all embedded images completing the look of the email.

Replying or Forwarding Formatted Emails

If you receive an RTF or HTML email that contains formatting, when you reply to it or forward it, the email retains all its formatting. However, the text you type in the Reply or Forward is in plain text. There is no way to add formatting to emails you type on your BlackBerry Curve.

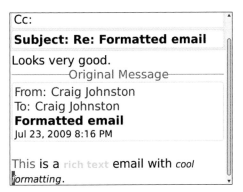

Shortcuts for Email Navigation

- Press the spacebar to scroll through an email page by page. Using the spacebar to page down saves on scrolling.

- Press the Shift and Space keys at the same time to page up in an email.

- Press B to go to the bottom of the list of messages.

- Press T to go to the top of the list.

- Press N to jump to the beginning of the next day of emails.

- Press P to jump to the beginning of the previous day of emails.

- Press U to jump to the next unread message.

- Press R to reply to the message.

- Press L to compose a Reply All to the message.

- Press F to forward the message.

- Press G to return to the spot in the email where you were before you closed it.

- Press J to go to the next email in the thread.

- Press K to go to the previous email in the thread.

Where Else Can I Use These Shortcuts?

The R, L, and F shortcuts also work in the message list while you have the message selected.

It's Not All Good

You cannot edit the original text of an email you are replying to or forwarding.

Change the Type of Messages Listed

You can change what type of messages are listed in the message list:

1. Press the Alt and I keys together to change the message list to display only incoming or received emails.

2. Press the Alt and O keys together to change the message list to display only outgoing or sent emails.

3. Press the Alt and P keys together to see only Phone Log messages.

4. Press the Alt and S keys together to see only SMS messages.

5. To compose a new message, press C.

>>>step-by-step

Email Cleanup, Searching, and Management

If you want to clean up email on your BlackBerry but do not want those emails to be deleted on your corporate or personal email accounts, you can delete messages in chunks by date:

1. Scroll to a specific date. Click the trackball or trackpad and choose Delete Prior. Your BlackBerry deletes all emails prior to that date.

2. To find text in an email, press the Menu key and choose Find.

3. Type in the word you want to find and press the Enter key. Your BlackBerry Curve searches the email you have open for that word.

4. If you want to find the next occurrence of that same word, press the Menu key and choose Find Next.

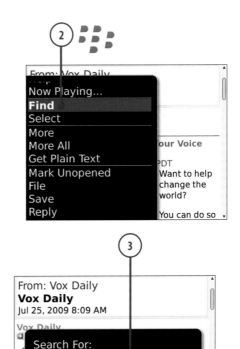

5. If you read a message and then decide you want to mark it as unread, scroll to the message in the message list. Click the Menu key and choose Mark Unopened.

6. To mark multiple messages as unread or unopened, hold the Shift key while scrolling with the trackball or trackpad. After they are selected, press the Menu key and choose Mark Unopened.

Repeat these steps to mark messages as read or opened.

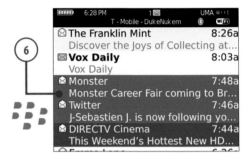

7. To mark all messages prior to a certain date as read or opened, scroll up to the date, press the Menu button, and choose Mark Prior Opened.

8. If you need to file a message to a specific folder, click the Menu key from the message list and choose File.

9. Scroll to the folder where you want to file the message. Click the trackball or trackpad to file the message.

Note

The list of folders is read from your personal or corporate mailbox; so when you file the message, it is moved to that folder on the mail server.

A message that has been filed shows the Folder icon instead of the Envelope icon.

Filed Message icon

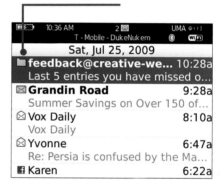

>>>step-by-step

Message Options

You can configure the Messages application to work the way you need it to.

1. To configure the Messages application, while running Messages, press the Menu key and choose Options.

You see the main Messages Options screen. Email Filters is listed only if you have a corporate BlackBerry.

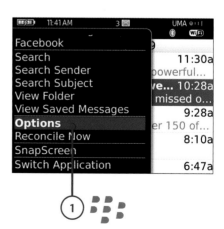

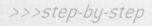

2. Click on General Options.

3. Display Time controls whether your BlackBerry displays the time that the message was received in the message list.

4. Display Name controls whether your BlackBerry displays the email senders' name in the message list.

5. Display Order controls whether your BlackBerry shows the sender's name and then the subject, or the subject first and then the sender's name in the message list.

6. Display Message Header On controls how many lines of the message header are shown in the message list. The message header is the Address fields and Subject line.

How Message Header Affects the Display

By default, the message header is set to two lines: The sender and the time the message was received are on the first line, and the message subject is on the second line.

If you change this setting to one line, the sender, subject, and time received are all on one line. Having them all on one line allows for more messages to fit onto the screen but shortens sender and subject length.

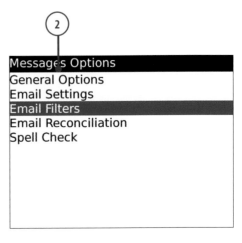

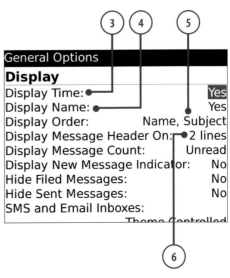

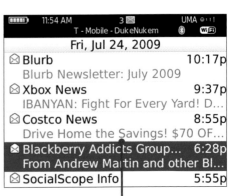

Display 2 lines per message

7. Display Message Count controls whether your BlackBerry Curve displays an icon at the top of the screen showing how many unread messages you have. Setting this to None turns this feature off.

8. Display New Message Indicator controls whether your BlackBerry Curve displays the red star next to the unread message indicator.

9. Hide Filed Messages controls whether your BlackBerry Curve hides a message after it has been filed in a folder other than the Inbox.

10. Hide Sent Messages controls whether your BlackBerry Curve hides a message after it has been sent.

Messages Are Not Deleted

When a message reaches the age you set, your BlackBerry deletes it. However, it is not deleted from your Inbox, because it is a maintenance event and not an actual delete.

Display 1 line per message

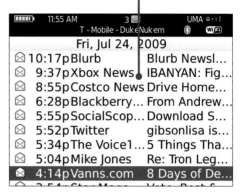

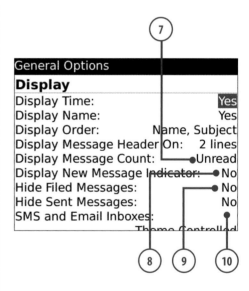

11. SMS and Email Inboxes controls whether the Messages application shows SMSs and emails. It can be set to Theme Controlled, which allows the theme you have selected to run on your BlackBerry to control this. You can override the Theme by selecting Combined or Separate.

12. Separators controls how emails are separated in the message list. You can set it to None, which is no separator, Stripes are where every second message in the list has a background color, and Lines are where a line separates the messages.

Under the Actions section, you have a few more options:

13. Make PIN Messages Level 1 tells your BlackBerry Curve to make any incoming PIN messages to Urgent or Level 1. This is useful if you have set up a special alert for Level 1 messages.

14. Auto More enables you to control whether your BlackBerry Curve automatically downloads more of a message if it is larger than 2K. If you set this to No, you need to manually choose to download more of a message when you get to the bottom and see the More line.

15. Confirm Delete controls whether your BlackBerry Curve prompts you when you choose to delete a message.

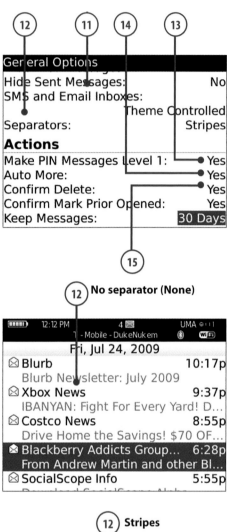

No separator (None)

Stripes

16. Confirm Mark Prior Opened controls whether your BlackBerry Curve prompts you when you choose to do a Mark Prior Opened.

17. Keep Messages enables you to control how long the BlackBerry Curve keeps your messages before deleting them. You can set this to 15 Days, 30 Days, 2 Months to 6 Months, or Forever.

>>>step-by-step

Corporate BlackBerry Email Settings

A corporate BlackBerry has a different Email Setting screen than a personal BlackBerry. It features four extra settings which only work on a BES.

1. Send Email To Handheld controls whether your corporate BES sends emails to your BlackBerry. If you set this to No, emails are no longer sent, but you can still send emails and browse the intranet.

2. Save Copy In Sent Folder controls whether emails that you compose and send on your BlackBerry are copied to the Sent folder in your corporate email client.

3. If you change Use Auto Signature to Yes, you can type in your email auto signature, which will be appended to all emails you send from your BlackBerry.

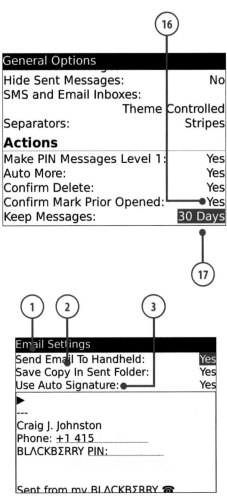

Signature Is Not Synchronized

The signature you enter on this screen is synchronized only to your BES. It is not synchronized with your corporate email signature.

4. If you change Use Out Of Office Reply to Yes, you can type a message that will be sent to people who email you while you are out of the office.

Out of Office Is Synchronized

The Out Of Office message you see on your BlackBerry is the same one you see in your corporate email program. Changes to this message on the BlackBerry are synchronized back to your corporate email program and vice versa.

Personal BlackBerry Email Settings

A personal BlackBerry has a different Email Setting screen than a corporate BlackBerry. It allows you to set email settings for each of your personal email accounts separately.

>>>step-by-step

1. If you have more than one email account on your BlackBerry, you see a line at the top of Email Settings called Message Services. You need to first make sure that the correct email account is selected before making any changes. For a corporate BlackBerry, one of the Message Services is called Desktop.

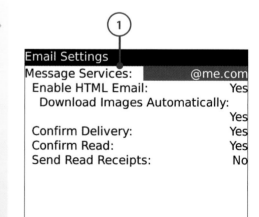

2. Enable HTML Email controls whether your BlackBerry downloads formatting for emails.

3. Download Images Automatically controls whether images embedded in emails are downloaded automatically.

4. Confirm Delivery enables you to configure your BlackBerry Curve to always request a delivery confirmation when sending email.

   If set to Yes, when an email you have sent is delivered, the Envelope icon next to the sent email shows a small D.

5. Confirm Read enables you to configure your BlackBerry Curve to always request a read receipt when sending email.

6. Send Read Receipts controls how your BlackBerry responds to read receipts. It can be set to Yes, No, or Prompt. Yes always sends back a Read Receipt if one is requested. No means that your BlackBerry never responds to a Read Request.

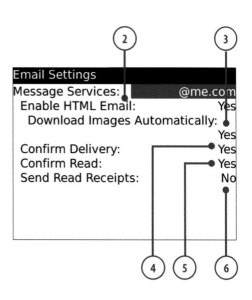

Delivery Receipt

In addition to the Read Receipt, any BlackBerry can send a Delivery Receipt. To make a BlackBerry send a Delivery Receipt no matter if its owner wants to or not, type **<confirm>** at the beginning of the subject line. Once that email is delivered to the BlackBerry, you will receive a return email confirming delivery.

It's Not All Good

Even when the Download Images Automatically option is set to Yes, the BlackBerry often does not download the images requiring you to choose Get Images in the menu to see them.

Email Filters

The next item in the Options list is Email Filters. This option is only available to corporate BlackBerry users who have a BlackBerry that is associated with the company's BlackBerry Enterprise Server.

When you open Email Filters, you might see some filters there already. This is because the BlackBerry Enterprise Server prepopulates at least two filters. This screen can filter out certain emails that you don't want on your BlackBerry. The emails will still be in your Inbox back at the office, but the BlackBerry Enterprise Server will not forward them to your BlackBerry Curve.

1. To create a new email filter, press the Menu button and choose New.

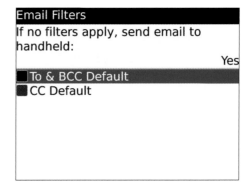

2. Type in a Filter Name.

3. Type in some unique information about the emails that you do not want forwarded to your BlackBerry. You can use one or more of the fields below the Filter Name, including From, Sent To, Subject, and Message.

    For example, if you do not want to see email from James Kirk, no matter what the email is about, type James Kirk in the From field.

4. If you do not want to see emails from James Kirk that have the subject of raise, type raise in the Subject field.

5. You can further clarify the filter by typing words in the Message field. This makes the filter trigger if the words you type in the Message field appear anywhere in the message body.

6. You can further clarify the filter by selecting extra criteria. For example, you might want a certain email to be forwarded to your BlackBerry if the email is sent to a Group; but if it is addressed to you directly, it must not be sent to your BlackBerry. To do this, check the Sent directly to me box.

7. The same applies to the Cc: to me and Bcc: to me.

8. You might want to filter out all emails and have only Urgent emails forwarded to you. To do this, you can change the Importance level.

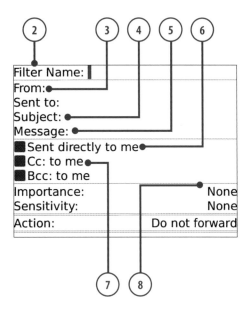

9. The same applies to the Sensitivity field.

10. The Action field controls whether the email is forwarded to your BlackBerry.

11. To save the filter, press the Escape key, and choose Save.

>>>step-by-step

Email Reconciliation

The next item on the Email Options screen is Email Reconciliation, which controls how emails are reconciled between your BlackBerry Curve and the email server.

1. If you have multiple email accounts, first select which one you want to modify by changing the Message Services field.

2. Delete On controls how emails are deleted. If you set it to Handheld, when you delete an email on your BlackBerry, that same email is not deleted on your mail server.

3. Wireless Reconcile controls whether your BlackBerry reconciles emails wirelessly. If you set this to No, your BlackBerry doesn't reconcile emails at all. It continues to receive emails wirelessly but no longer reconciles them.

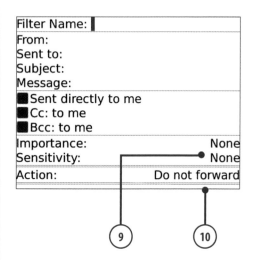

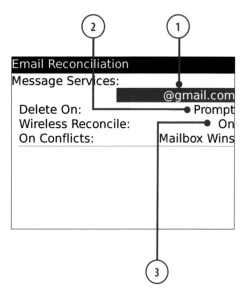

Delete On Choices

If you set this to Mailbox & Handheld, when you delete an email on your BlackBerry, that same email is deleted on your mail server. The reverse is also true. If you delete an email on your mail server, that same email is deleted from your BlackBerry.

If you set this option to Prompt, each time you delete an email on your BlackBerry, you are prompted where to make that deletion.

4. On Conflicts enables you to set who wins when there is a conflict between your mail server and your BlackBerry. The choices are Mailbox Wins and Handheld Wins. Setting it to Mailbox Wins, for example, means that if something changes on a particular email on your BlackBerry and your mail server, the email on the mail server replaces the one on your BlackBerry.

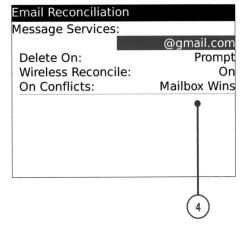

Spell Check

The last item on the Email Options list is Spell Check. This screen controls the way your BlackBerry Curve handles spell-checking emails.

1. Ignore Case tells your BlackBerry to ignore the case of words when it checks them.

2. Ignore Acronyms tells your BlackBerry to ignore words that it identifies as common acronyms.

3. Ignore Words With Numbers tells your BlackBerry not to attempt to spell check words you type that contain numbers.

4. Spell Check Email Before Sending enables you to make your BlackBerry spell check your email again before you send it. This setting is only useful if you turn off Check Spelling As You Type (the next option).

5. Check Spelling As You Type tells your BlackBerry to continually check your spelling as you type. If you turn this off, you need to turn on the previous option if you still want to spell check before you actually send the email.

6. Minimum Sized Word To Check tells your BlackBerry the number of letters a word must be to spell check it. The default is two letters.

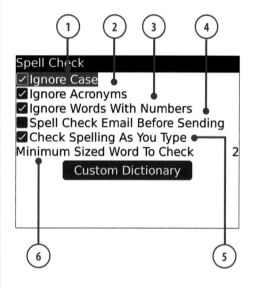

7. If you click on the Custom Dictionary, you see any words that have been added to your BlackBerry's custom dictionary.

8. You can add new words to it by pressing the Menu key and choosing New. Type in the new custom word, and press Enter.

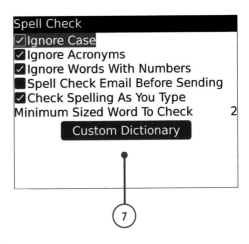

Spell Check
☑ Ignore Case
☑ Ignore Acronyms
☑ Ignore Words With Numbers
■ Spell Check Email Before Sending
☑ Check Spelling As You Type
Minimum Sized Word To Check   2

Custom Dictionary

7

Taking Your Custom Dictionary with You

If you make use of the custom dictionary, make sure you back up your BlackBerry often because if you need to switch BlackBerrys, the custom dictionary is restored from the backup.

Synchronizing BlackBerry Email Via a Mac

PocketMac for BlackBerry offers two unique features that might appeal to you.

>>>*step-by-step*

PocketMac for BlackBerry Email Synchronization

The Email option enables you to synchronize your BlackBerry Curve's Inbox or Sent folders with your Mac.

1. Start PocketMac for BlackBerry.

2. Connect your BlackBerry Curve via the USB cable.

3. Click the BlackBerry icon to configure PocketMac for BlackBerry.

4. Click the Email tab.

5. Check the box next to Copy BlackBerry inbox/sent messages to.

6. Select which email program you want to copy the messages to.

7. Click the Advanced Preferences button.

8. Choose whether you want the received email on your BlackBerry to synchronize with the Inbox.

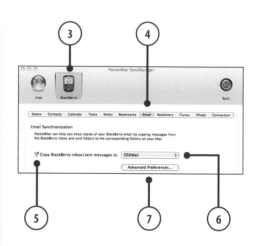

Is It Needed?

This is not normally necessary because most POP3 and IMAP email servers keep the Inbox up to date, so there would be a copy of the received email in both places already.

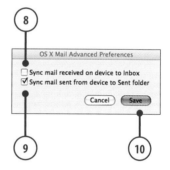

9. Choose whether you want the sent email on your BlackBerry to synchronize with the Sent folder.

It Can Be Very Useful

This is useful because almost no mail servers synchronize the Sent items. For example, if you send an email from your BlackBerry, that email will be in the Sent folder on your BlackBerry but not on your mail server.

10. Click the Save button.

Email Redelivery

PocketMac for BlackBerry allows for email redelivery. This feature puts email that was received on your Mac on your BlackBerry so you can respond from your BlackBerry.

The Redelivery option enables you to have email forwarded to your BlackBerry while your Mac is turned on. This is useful if you do not use a POP3 or IMAP email server, or if you use corporate email and your company does not have a BlackBerry Enterprise Server. By leaving your Mac turned on, it can act as a mini-BlackBerry server. The only drawback is that your Mac has to stay powered on all the time.

1. Click on the Redelivery tab.

2. Check the box next to Forward my new incoming email from.

3. Select the mail service to forward from.

4. If you want this to work only when you are away from your Mac, check the box next to Only forward email when I'm away from my Mac.

5. Enter your BlackBerry's email address.

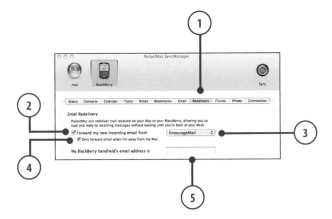

In this chapter, you learn about surfing the web on your BlackBerry Curve. Topics include the following:

→ Configuring the BlackBerry Browser
→ Surfing the web using different screen layouts
→ Exploring the purpose of the different BlackBerry Browsers

6

Surfing the Web

Browsing the Internet on a smartphone can sometimes be frustrating because of the way the web browser changes the layout of pages. The BlackBerry Browser can handle websites and can render them almost perfectly, enabling you more of a desktop web browsing experience.

Your BlackBerry Curve web browser can be used to browse Internet websites and your company's intranet websites if you are using a corporate BlackBerry. The browser supports many web technologies including embedded images, rich text, links to documents, and embedded videos similar to the way YouTube works.

To open the web browser, from the BlackBerry Home Screen, click Browser.

Click to launch the browser

The Different BlackBerry Browsers

Your BlackBerry attempts to provide the greatest flexibility when browsing the web by offering a web browser for every occasion. In reality, you will probably use only one of them, but it is good to know what each one is for.

BlackBerry Browser

If you have a BlackBerry Curve that is on your company's BlackBerry Enterprise Server (BES), you have the BlackBerry Browser. When you browse the web using the BlackBerry Browser, you are actually browsing through your company's BES, onto its intranet and out onto the web.

This enables you to access internal company websites that might exist on your intranet. This is a powerful feature of your BlackBerry because it enables you to access internal company information while you are on the road.

This method of access is also completely secure because your web browsing session is encrypted from your BlackBerry all the way to your company's BES. In some cases your BlackBerry Administrator might allow you to use only the BlackBerry Browser and block all the other ones for security reasons.

When you browse the web using the BlackBerry Browser, you are not actually accessing the web pages directly, but rather your BlackBerry makes the request for the pages, and the BES retrieves them on your behalf. This is commonly known as a proxy, and in this case the BES acts as your web proxy.

Data Path for BlackBerry Browser

BlackBerry <-> Wireless Carrier <-> RIM NOC <-> BES <-> Intranet <-> Internet

---

Internet Browser

The Internet Browser is the default browser for BlackBerry users who are not on a company BES and have a personal BlackBerry. The Internet Browser doesn't enable browsing to websites on a company intranet, but rather you can use it for direct Internet browsing.

In reality, the Internet Browser still uses a BlackBerry Server called the BlackBerry Internet Server (BIS). This server is hosted either on the RIM network or the wireless carrier's network. All personal BlackBerrys connect to a BIS.

Like the BlackBerry Browser, when you browse the web using the Internet Browser, you do not access the web directly. The BIS is acting as a proxy for you and fetching the web pages on your behalf.

Data Path for Internet Browser

BlackBerry <-> Wireless Carrier <-> RIM NOC <-> BIS <-> Internet

---

WAP Browser

WAP stands for Wireless Access Protocol and was an early technology used to browse the web from a mobile phone. WAP Browsers do not understand regular web pages, so special websites are needed that use a technology called Wireless Markup Language (WML).

The benefit of special mobile websites that use WML are that the sites load quickly, and the pages are formatted for small screens. Loading these mobile sites doesn't use up large amounts of data. All this was important many years ago when browsing the Internet from a mobile phone was slow and expensive, not to mention the screens were very small.

WAP browsing and WAP sites are not that prevalent now when most carriers offer unlimited data plans, and the 3G wireless networks offer decent Internet access speeds. WAP is still supported by many wireless carriers, so this browser is there for that support.

To support WAP, a wireless carrier uses a WAP Gateway. The purpose of this gateway is to limit what websites you can access from your mobile phone and convert any web pages that are not in WML to WML format on-the-fly.

On your BlackBerry Curve, the WAP Browser might not be called the WAP
Browser. Your carrier might have renamed it. For example, if you have a
BlackBerry Curve on T-Mobile US's network, the WAP Browser is called
T-Mobile.

Data Path for WAP Browser

BlackBerry <-> Wireless Carrier <-> WAP Gateway <-> Internet

Hotspot Browser

If your BlackBerry Curve has a Wi-Fi radio, you can also see the Hotspot
Browser. This browser connects directly to Wi-Fi Hotspots and accesses the
Internet directly. The Wi-Fi Hotspot can be anywhere—at your home, in a
coffee shop, at an airport, and so on.

In most cases, the Wi-Fi Browser enables direct Internet browsing through a
Hotspot, but in certain situations your wireless carrier might force the
Hotspot Browser through the BIS.

Data Path for Hotspot Browser

BlackBerry <-> Hotspot <-> Internet

Now that you know about the different browsers, select any one you like, and
let's go through the settings. We choose the default browser in the next section, which is the browser that your BlackBerry Curve always tries to use first,
so when making the selection here, choose that browser.

>>>*step-by-step*

Configuring the Browser

Before we actually browse the web,
let's first configure the BlackBerry
Curve's web browser to work the way
we want it to.

1. Click Menu, and choose Options.

Browser to Configure

This screen enables you to configure your browser. At the top of the screen, you see a Browser field. Click the choices to see a list of browsers. Each browser can be configured differently.

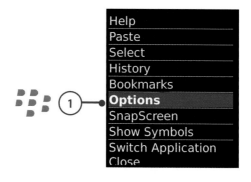

2. When in the Options screen, click Browser Configuration.

3. Select the browser you want to configure.

4. The first is Support JavaScript. Check the box to enable JavaScript support.

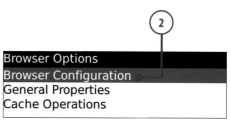

5. The next setting is Prompt to Enable JavaScript. This tells your BlackBerry to prompt you to enable JavaScript if a website requires it. For now leave this box checked.

6. Next is Show Images; leave this setting enabled because it tells your BlackBerry to load images on web pages. Since many websites use images for navigation, you normally need to leave this enabled.

7. Next is Use Background Images, which tells your BlackBerry to make use of web page background images. Leave this enabled for the most complete web browsing experience.

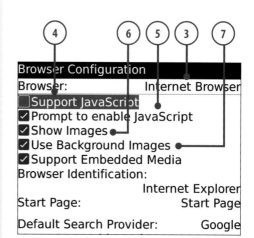

8. Next is Support Embedded Media, which are audio or video files. Many websites have embedded videos that you can play on the web page. If you leave this option enabled, you can actually browse to sites like YouTube and play videos directly.

9. The next setting is Browser Identification, which can be confusing because after all are you not using a BlackBerry? Why would you not want to identify yourself as a BlackBerry user? See the next section for a complete explanation.

10. The next setting is the Start Page. You can change it to display the Bookmarks Page, Home Page, Last Page Loaded, or Start Page.

11. The next setting is Default Search Provider. That enables you to set which search engine or provider you want to use anytime you perform a search. This sets the search provider for the Start Page.

12. The final setting is Home Page Address that enables you to set your browser home page. You can type in the address manually or click Use Current to use the web page you are currently on as your home page.

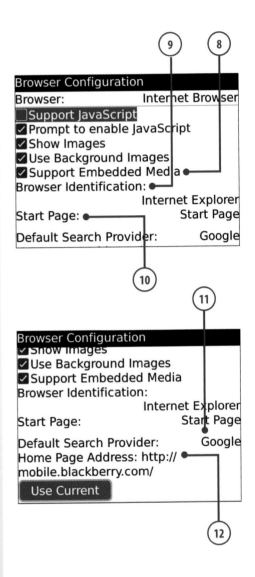

How Are Videos Played?

When you click a video to play it, your BlackBerry exits the browser and launches the Media Player. The video then starts playing in the Media Player. When you exit the video, you return to the web page.

It's Not All Good

JavaScript is a script that is embedded in a web page that your web browser runs. You can use JavaScript for many things such as page formatting or even reading your GPS location. The BlackBerry can process JavaScript, but in many cases it takes a long time to do so. Although RIM has a fix for this, it is recommended that you uncheck this feature.

Browser Identification Explained

We have to take a little detour to explain this. Way back when mobile browsing was still getting started, mobile phones had tiny screens and slow Internet connections. Because of this, WML was invented, as we discussed earlier, which led to stripped down websites.

Later when smartphones arrived, mobile web browsing slowly started to get better and better. Internet connection speeds got faster and mobile phone screen sizes got larger. In conjunction with this, website designers started using a technique of figuring out what kind of device was accessing their sites. They can do this because when you request to open a web page, your device actually sends the web server some information that includes the name of your web browser.

This is very useful to website designers because based on what they see, they can redirect you to a version of their website that is more suitable for your device.

So for example, if a web server receives a request to open a page and it sees that the request is coming from Internet Explorer, Firefox, or Safari, it assumes that these are desktop computers. If it sees that the request is coming from Pocket Internet Explorer or BlackBerry, it assumes that these are smartphones and redirects the page request to a mobile friendly version of their site. The mobile friendly version of the site does not necessarily need to be using WML, it can use regular HTML; however, the site will be designed with the mobile device in mind. Screen sizes will be smaller, less graphics will be used, and a simpler layout of the content will be employed.

This redirection based on device type was very successful for many years and provided mobile phone users access to websites that would just be too painfully slow to load normally, and too difficult to navigate on a small screen.

Now, however, we have a situation where mobile browsers on smartphones are much more sophisticated and are very close to being as good as web browsers on regular computers. The dilemma then is how to get around the web servers' decision-making process. The way to do this is to pretend to be something that you are not.

If you are on your BlackBerry Curve, the Browser Identification is set to BlackBerry, and you browse to CNN.com, you will notice that you do not see the regular CNN website. This is because the CNN website saw that you requested the page from a BlackBerry and it redirected you to a completely different CNN website at m.cnn.com. This website is specifically designed for mobile devices.

Now if you change the Browser Identification to Firefox and go back to CNN.com you will notice that the CNN web site now looks very similar to the way it does on your computer.

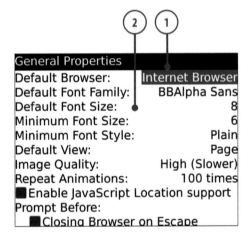

>>>*step-by-step*

Browser General Properties

This section allows you to configure the general properties of the BlackBerry Browser. These properties are global.

1. Default Browser tells your BlackBerry which browser to try to use first. For now, let's leave it on Internet Browser.

2. Default Font Family and Font Size enable you to choose the default font that the web browser uses if a website does not specify one. If you have a hard time reading small screens, you might want to increase the font size.

3. Minimum Font Size and Font Style enables you to override what a website tries to set the font to. This allows you to avoid fonts that are too small to be readable.

4. The Default View controls how the website is rendered on the screen. The default is Page. The other choice is Column.

5. Next is Image Quality that controls what your BlackBerry does when it needs to load an image or images on a web page. It is set to Medium by default, but you can set it to Low or High.

6. The Enable JavaScript Location Support setting is off by default. You might want to enable it if you want some websites to query where you are. Some website functions might be enhanced by knowing your location.

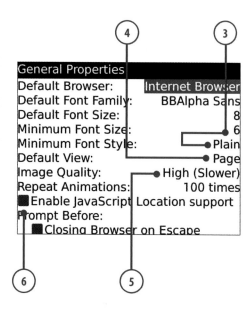

General Properties

Default Browser:	Internet Browser
Default Font Family:	BBAlpha Sans
Default Font Size:	8
Minimum Font Size:	6
Minimum Font Style:	Plain
Default View:	Page
Image Quality:	High (Slower)
Repeat Animations:	100 times

■ Enable JavaScript Location support
Prompt Before:
   ■ Closing Browser on Escape

Page Versus Column

If you leave the setting to Page and you browse the Internet, the BlackBerry keeps the page layout the same as the web designer intended it to be. This means that when you browse to a web page, you see the entire horizontal footprint of the web page zoomed out to fit your BlackBerry's screen. This enables you to scroll around the page with the trackball or trackpad; then click to zoom in on a part of the page you want to read more closely. In addition, you cannot click anything until you zoom in at least once.

If you set this to Column, your BlackBerry reformats the page so that everything is in a long column. The idea of this view is that the contents of the page are already zoomed to a comfortable reading level, and you don't need to scroll left and right like you would have to on the Page view when zoomed in. In addition, unlike the Page view, you can immediately click links without first having to zoom in. Although this is a good idea, the drawback is that the BlackBerry reformats the page, and it no longer looks exactly like it does on your desktop.

Effects of Changing Image Quality

If you set this to High, your BlackBerry always loads the full image. The drawback is that image loading can take longer and use up more data. The middle of the road choice is Medium. When set to Medium your BlackBerry won't load the full image but just enough to render a medium-quality version of it. In most cases this is OK, but if you want to see the website in all its glory and you have an unlimited data plan, set this to High. In fact if you change the browser at the top to Hotspot Browser, it makes sense to set this to High because you will be browsing on a Wi-Fi Hotspot and therefore a very fast connection making this even more appropriate.

⑦

```
General Properties
Minimum Font Style:              Plain
Default View:                     Page
Image Quality:          High (Slower)
Repeat Animations:          100 times
■ Enable JavaScript Location support
Prompt Before:
   ■ Closing Browser on Escape
   ☑ Closing Modified Pages
   ☑ Switching to WAP for streaming
     media
   ☐ Running WML Scripts
```

7. The last few settings control when you must be prompted. For example, you might want to be prompted if you press the Escape key to exit the browser.

Browser Cache Properties

The final Options category is Cache Properties, which is a screen that enables you to clear your browser history, Content Cache, Pushed Content, and Cookie Cache. Your browser history is a running log of the websites you have visited.

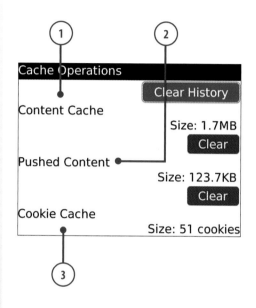

1. The Cache stores images and other content from web pages you have visited. If you return to a website that is using the same files, your Blackberry will find them in your cache so it does not need to load them over the air. This helps speed up web page loading and reduce data costs.

2. Pushed Content is usually used only when your BlackBerry is on your company's BES. Sometimes web pages are pushed to your device.

3. Finally, Cookies are little files placed in memory by websites that track you and enhance your browsing experience by putting settings in these files.

Why Clear the Cache?

You might want to clear this information for many reasons. One reason might be not wanting people to know where you have been browsing if they happen to pick up your BlackBerry, but another reason might just be to clear up a bit of extra memory.

Using the Web Browser

Now that you have set all the options for your Browser, let's actually browse the web.

Browser Start Page

When you open the web browser, you are normally presented with the Start Page unless you changed this in the options. The Start page shows the address bar, search bar, Bookmarks, and History on the same page. This is useful because it is likely that you want to search for something or just click a website you visited previously in the Bookmarks or History.

Because the Bookmarks and History sections on the Start Page show only a short version of your actual Bookmarks and History, to see the full list of each, simply click the name Bookmarks or History.

>>>*step-by-step*

1. If you click Bookmarks, you see all your Bookmarks listed in Categories. The actual bookmarks that you add are under a heading of BlackBerry Bookmarks.

2. If you escape back to the Start Page, click History. This will show all of your browser history. You will see a heading for Today and previous days of the week.

Bookmark Headings

The other headings are normally pre-populated by RIM and your wireless carrier. The other categories or headings should be Links; Carrier Bookmarks (instead of the word carrier, you should see your carrier's name, for example, T-Mobile Bookmarks); WiFi Services (if you have a Wi-Fi enabled BlackBerry Curve); and sometimes a heading with just your carrier's name, for example, T-Mobile.

3. If you expand a particular day by clicking it, the list expands to show the websites that you visited on that day.

4. If you expand a particular website, you can see the different web pages on that website that you visited.

Why Use History?

Browsing through the history can sometimes help you find a web page you remembered accessing on a particular day but cannot quite remember its name or where in the site you saw what you are looking for. Having it all listed out like this can be very helpful.

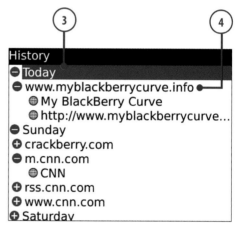

>>>*step-by-step*

Browsing the Web

Let's go to a website. So that web-sites do not identify your BlackBerry as a mobile device, set the Browser Identification to Internet Explorer. This provides the richest browsing experience and the closest to browsing on a desktop computer.

1. Click the Browser icon from the BlackBerry Home screen.

2. Click Menu, and choose Options.

3. Click Browser Configuration.

4. Scroll down to Browser Identification, and change it to Internet Explorer.

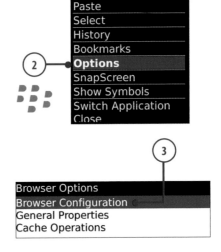

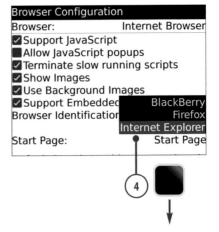

5. Press the Escape key, and choose Save.

6. Press the Escape key once more to return to the Browser Starts page.

7. On the Start Page, click in the address bar, and start typing **cnn.com**. The http://www part is already there.

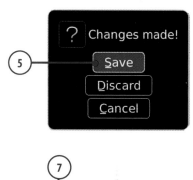

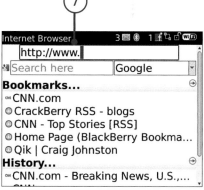

You Don't Need to Type the Period

When typing a web address in a field in which your BlackBerry is expecting a web address, you don't need to use the period. Your BlackBerry knows that you are typing a web address and knows ahead of time that web addresses never have spaces and always have periods.

To type a period on your BlackBerry Curve keyboard, you need to hold the Alt key to get to the alternative character on the M key that is the period. Because of this, to make it quicker to type web addresses, you do not need to type the period; just press space instead of the period. Here's an example.

If you need to type in the website www.cnn.com, you actually type **www** <space> **cnn** <space> **com**. The BlackBerry replaces the <space> with a period so that the end result on the screen is www.cnn.com.

8. After you type in www.cnn.com, press Enter, and the browser starts to load the page. If you are in Page view, you see your BlackBerry website looking almost exactly like it does on your computer.

9. Click the trackball or trackpad to zoom in on the page. Now your magnifying glass cursor becomes a mouse pointer.

10. If you still have a hard time reading the page, click Menu, and choose Zoom In. This zooms in a bit more.

You can now browse the web as you would on a desktop computer. The pointer that you can scroll in all directions using the trackball or trackpad looks like a mouse pointer and changes to a Pointing Hand icon when you scroll over a link that can be clicked. To click the link, just click the trackball or trackpad.

To go back one page, press Escape.

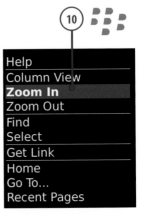

11. To copy a part of a web page, click Menu, and choose Select.

12. Scroll over the part of the website you want to copy.

13. Click Menu and choose Copy.

Where Can You Paste the Selected Text?

You can now paste the copied content into emails, MemoPad entries, or anywhere. In most cases the pasted content loses its formatting and reverts back to plain text.

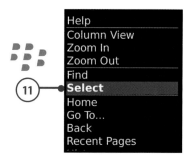

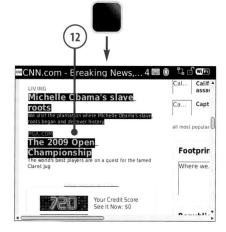

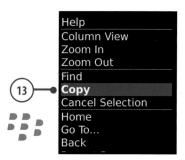

14. To send the address of the web page you are on, press Menu, and choose Send Address.

15. Then choose the method you want to send the address. These include Email, PIN, SMS Text, MMS, and Messenger Contact.

16. If you want to save an image on a web page to your BlackBerry Curve, hover the pointer over the image.

17. Press Menu and choose Save Image.

18. You can see the pictures folder on your BlackBerry. Click Save to save the image.

19. To save a copy of the web page to your BlackBerry Curve, press Menu and choose Save Page.

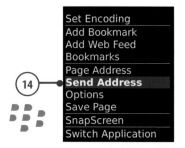

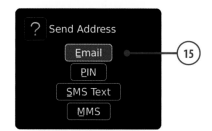

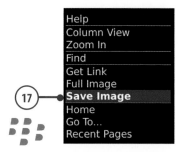

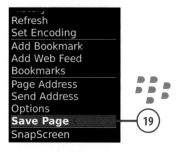

20. Click OK to save the page to your Messages. When you open your Messages view, you see the web page among your emails. The web page has a Globe icon instead of an Envelope icon.

>>>*step-by-step*

Bookmarking Websites

Just like a desktop web browser, you might want to bookmark this website. Your BlackBerry bookmarking process not only enables you to bookmark a page, but also to make it available offline.

1. While viewing a web page, press Menu and choose Add Bookmark.

2. In the Name field, you might want to shorten the name. Backspace to delete the part of the name you want to delete.

3. The Folder field enables you to place the bookmark in a specific folder and even create a new folder for this bookmark. Creating or using folders helps you keep bookmarks organized.

4. Available Offline is unchecked by default. If you did want to have access to this page while you are out of coverage, check this box.

5. If you chose to have this web page available offline, this is where you select how often your BlackBerry Curve must refresh the page contents. Change Auto Synchronize to something other than Never.

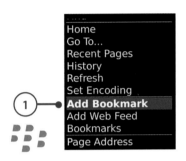

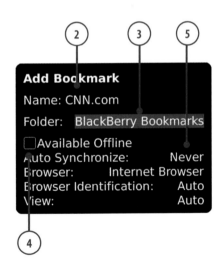

Can You Look at Pages Without Coverage?

Having a website available for offline viewing can be useful for situations where you are flying or in tunnels in which there is no coverage but you still want to see the contents of the site. The contents of the page are loaded into memory so that they can be retrieved later.

6. The Browser field enables you to preset which of the web browsers are used when opening this Bookmark.

7. Browser Identification enables you to preset how your BlackBerry will identify itself when you access this bookmark. Leaving this set to Auto means that your current browser setting will be used. To override the current setting, change this to BlackBerry, Firefox, or Internet Explorer.

8. View enables you to preset which browser view is used when opening this bookmark. Leaving this set to Auto means that your current browser setting will be used. To override the current setting, change this to either Column or Page.

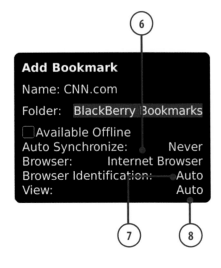

9. JavaScript enables you to preset whether JavaScript is enabled or disabled when accessing this bookmark. Leaving this set to Auto means that your current browser setting will be used. To override the current setting, change this to Enabled or Disabled.

10. Click Add to save and add this bookmark.

What Is RSS?

RSS originally stood for Rich Site Summary but was later renamed to Really Simple Syndication. It is a mechanism that enables someone to subscribe to a feed of the content of a website. The feed is updated in real time when new stories or content are added to the website. Your computer or BlackBerry can be set to update the RSS feed at regular intervals, and if there is new content, it downloads it.

This enables someone to stay in touch with a website's updates without having to open a browser and visit the site.

Subscribe to RSS Feeds

Many blogs and websites now use RSS feeds to enable their visitors to stay up to date on the contents of their sites without having to browse there.

1. To subscribe to a Web Feed, open a website that you know has one or more RSS feeds.

2. Press Menu and choose Add Web Feed.

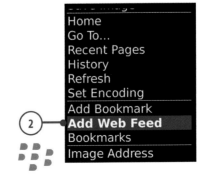

3. You see a list of web feeds or RSS feeds available on that website. Put a check mark next to the feeds you want to subscribe to.

4. Choose the folder you want the web feeds to be stored in.

5. Choose whether to Auto Synchronize the web feeds. If you leave this set to Never, your BlackBerry will update only the feeds when you click the web feed in the bookmarks screen. If you want your BlackBerry to update the web feeds on a regular basis, change this to a value other than Never.

6. The Browser field enables you to preset which of the web browsers are used when opening this Bookmark.

7. Click Add to save and add this web feed.

8. To view a web feed, go to your Bookmarks and click the Web Feed. The stories in that feed will be listed on the screen.

9. If you use the trackball or track-pad to click one of the stories, you see a screen that asks if you want to Show Description or Read Story. If you choose Show Description, the screen expands to show you a preview of the story.

10. If you choose Read Story, the full story opens in the browser.

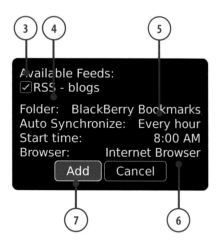

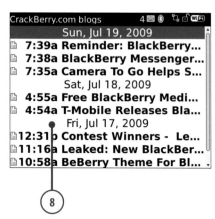

It's Not All Good

Unfortunately, if you want to go back to edit a Web Feed, you will find that it is no longer called a Web Feed, but rather a Bookmark. Keep this in mind when trying to edit your feeds.

>>>step-by-step

Searching Using the Web Browser

Although you could type in the address of your favorite Internet search engine, the BlackBerry Browser can search for you.

1. When you open the web browser and it shows the Start Page, under the address field there is a search field. On the right of the search field, you see a drop-down field that enables you to choose the search engine to use. Click that field and make your choice.

2. After you choose your search engine, the logo to the left of the search field changes to reflect that search engine. Type in your search string, and press Enter.

3. The BlackBerry Browser runs the search against your search engine of choice and shows you the results.

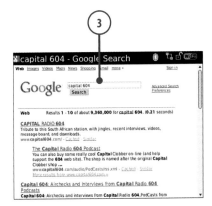

>>>step-by-step

Browsing with Only Wi-Fi Coverage

What if you are in an area that has only Wi-Fi coverage and no cellular coverage? You can still browse the web because your BlackBerry Curve detects that no coverage exists and switches to the Hotspot Browser. If you want to manually set the HotSpot Browser to be the default browser, follow these steps:

1. Press Menu, and choose Options.

2. On the Browser Options screen, choose General Properties.

3. Change the Default Browser to Hotspot Browser.

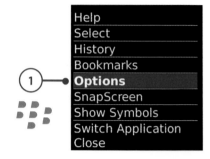

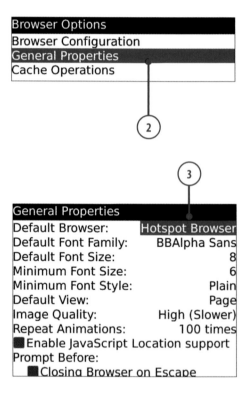

4. Press Escape, and choose Save.

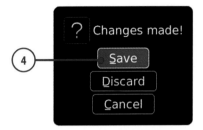

Hotspot Browser May Be Blocked

If you have a corporate BlackBerry, your BlackBerry Administrator might choose to block the Hotspot browser using an IT Policy. Unfortunately, if it is blocked and you have no cellular coverage, you cannot browse the Internet unless your BlackBerry Curve supports UMA, as we previously discussed.

Volume

Media Player

Camera

In this chapter, you learn about text messaging (SMS) and multimedia messaging (MMS) on your BlackBerry Curve. Topics include the following:

→ Configuring text messaging sound
→ Sending and receiving text and multimedia messages
→ BlackBerry PIN messages

Text Messaging, Multimedia Messaging, and BlackBerry PIN Messaging

Short Message Service (SMS) or text messaging has been available for mobile phones since 1993 and Multimedia Messaging Service (MMS) since 2002. Text messaging has been popular for a long time and has almost become the default method of communication for young people. Multimedia messaging is a newer technology, but it too is becoming more used. The BlackBerry Curve supports both SMS and MMS plus an additional text messaging format called BlackBerry PIN messages. We cover all three in this chapter.

>>>*step-by-step*

Configuring the New Text Message Sound

You might want to change the sound that is played when you receive a new text message. This helps set your BlackBerry Curve apart from the crowd.

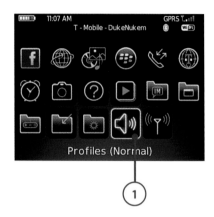

Profiles (Normal)

1. From the BlackBerry Home Screen, click Profiles.

Alternative Profiles Icon

If you are on the Today Screen, you will normally find the Profiles icon on the top left of the screen just under the battery indicator.

Alternative Profiles icon

2. On the Profile Select screen, select Advanced to edit the Profiles.

3. Scroll to the Profile that you want to edit; press Menu, and choose Edit.

4. Scroll through the list of alert types until you reach SMS Text. Click to edit.

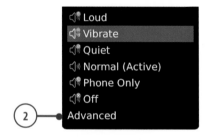

Loud
Vibrate
Quiet
Normal (Active)
Phone Only
Off
Advanced

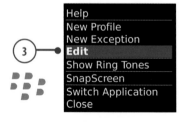

Help
New Profile
New Exception
Edit
Show Ring Tones
SnapScreen
Switch Application
Close

5. Scroll down to Ring Tone, and
   click to change the sound played
   for your incoming SMSs.

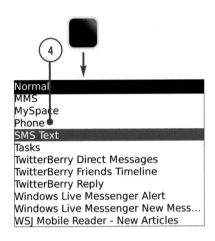

Two Places to Change the Ring Tone

Remember from our previous discussion in Chapter 1, "Making, Receiving, and Managing Calls," this screen enables you to configure what your BlackBerry does when it is in or out of a holster or a case.

6. To select music or a ring tone that
   you loaded, scroll to the top of the
   list, and click Browse.

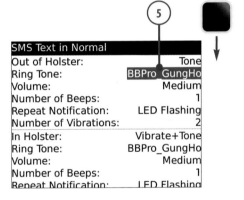

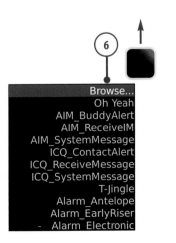

7. If you do choose to browse, you will see the audio folder layout of your BlackBerry. Browse through the folders until your find the song, ring tone, or other audio file you want to use as a ring tone.

8. After you select the sound or song you want to play when you receive a new incoming SMS, scroll down to the In Holster section, and make a change there.

9. Change the Notify Me During Calls to Yes if you want your BlackBerry Curve to alert you of incoming SMSs while you are on a phone call. Change to No if not.

10. Press Escape, and choose Save to save your changes.

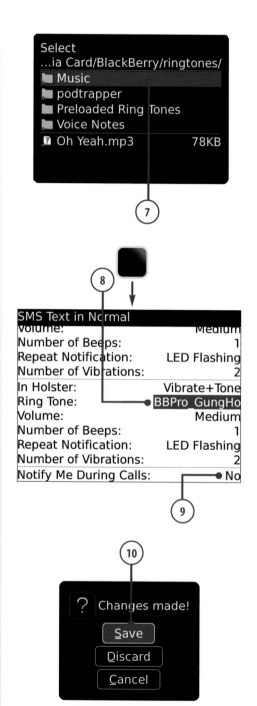

Sending SMS Text Messages

1. Depending on the Theme you use on your BlackBerry Curve, you might have a separate SMS and MMS icon on the BlackBerry Home Screen. You can click on either one to send an SMS.

2. To send an SMS, press Menu, and choose Compose SMS Text.

3. Start typing the name of the person you want to send the SMS to. If he or she is not in your address book, simply enter his or her mobile phone number. You can add multiple recipients so that you can send the same SMS to multiple people.

Multiple Charges

If you send an SMS to multiple people, you are charged for each recipient.

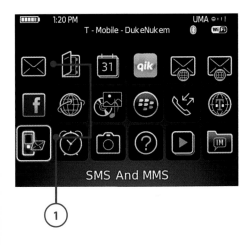

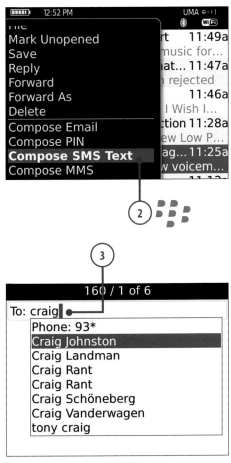

4. Type your SMS text message.

What Happens to Long Texts

If you type a message that is longer that 160 characters, don't worry because your BlackBerry simply breaks up your message and sends the messages as separate SMSs. The numbers at the top represent how many characters remain in that SMS, whereas the 1 of 6 represents the number of separate SMSs the BlackBerry has broken your message up into.

5. To send your SMS, press the trackball or trackpad, and choose Send.

>>>step-by-step

SMS Delivery Reports

You can request a delivery report when the SMS you send arrives on the recipient's mobile phone.

1. While composing a new SMS or reply to an SMS, press Menu, and choose Options.

2. Change the Delivery Report field to On.

3. Press Escape, and choose Save to save the changes.

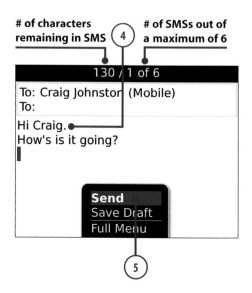

# of characters remaining in SMS ④ # of SMSs out of a maximum of 6

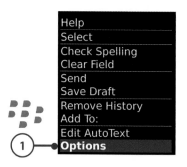

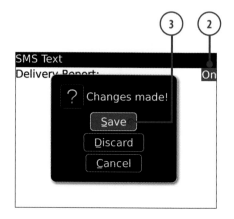

4. When the SMS arrives on the recipient's mobile phone, a small D will be added to the sent message's icon in the message list.

>>>step-by-step

Receiving and Replying to SMS Text Messages

Depending on the Theme you use, you might have a separate SMS and MMS icon on the BlackBerry Home Screen that indicates new SMSs.

1. When you receive a new SMS, it is listed in the message list. You will notice that the icon is slightly different from an email icon.

2. To read the SMS, click it with the trackball or trackpad. Notice that the view is set up so that you can follow the SMS conversation.

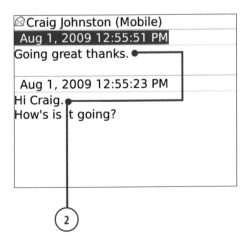

3. To reply to the SMS, click the trackball or trackpad, and choose Reply. Type your reply. Notice that the conversational layout of the screen remains, so you can see the entire thread.

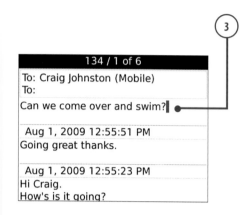

> >>>step-by-step

Configuring the New Multimedia Message Sound

You might want to change the sound that is played when you receive a new multimedia message.

1. From the BlackBerry Home Screen, click Profiles, or from the BlackBerry Today Screen, click the speaker icon in the top-left part of the screen.

2. On the Profile Select screen, select Advanced to edit the Profiles.

3. Scroll to the Profile that you want to edit; press Menu, and choose Edit.

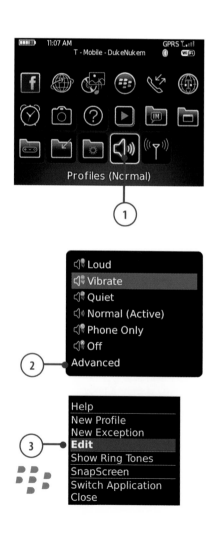

4. Scroll through the list of alert types until you reach MMS. Click to edit.

5. Remember from our previous discussion in Chapter 1 that this screen enables you to configure what the BlackBerry does when it is in and out of a holster or case. Scroll down to Ring Tone, and click to change the sound played for your incoming MMSs.

6. To select music or a ring tone that you loaded, scroll to the top of the list, and click Browse.

7. If you choose to browse, you will see the audio folder structure on your BlackBerry. Select any song, ring tone, or other audio file.

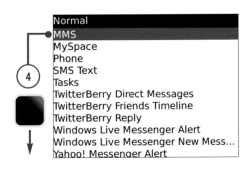

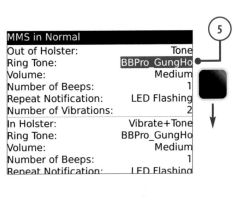

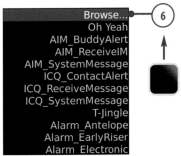

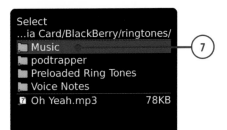

8. After you select the sound or song you want to play when you receive a new incoming MMS, scroll down to the In Holster section, and make a change there if you want to.

9. Change the Notify Me During Calls to Yes if you want your BlackBerry Curve to alert you of incoming MMSs while you are on a phone call. Change to No if not.

10. Press Escape, and choose Save to save your changes.

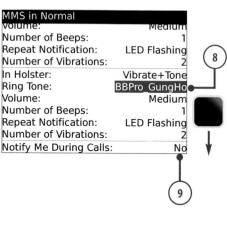

>>>*step-by-step* ▶

Sending Multimedia Messages from the Messages Application

Multimedia messages are messages that can be sent with multimedia attachments. Because of this, you can compose and send an MMS from the Messages application or browse to the file you want to send, and send it directly from there.

With the exception of pictures, the files you attach to MMS messages must be under 300K. Your BlackBerry scales down a picture so that it is under 300K before it sends it.

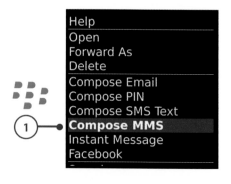

1. From the Messages application, press Menu and choose Compose MMS.

2. Select the person or persons you want to send the MMS to from the address book.

3. You can type a subject and some text in the body of the message.

4. To attach one or more files, press Menu, and choose either Attach Picture, Audio, Video, or Voice Note.

5. You can browse your BlackBerry's memory or your external media card for the files you want to attach. Scroll over the file you want to be attached and click the trackball or trackpad.

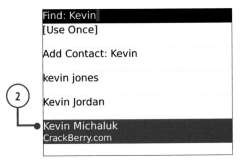

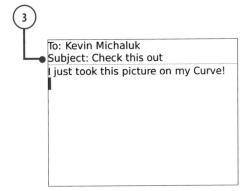

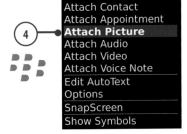

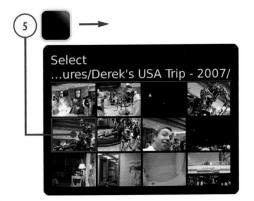

6. After the files are attached, you can interact with them in the message. For example, if you attach a picture, you see the picture in the message body. If you have attached audio or video, you can play it right in the message.

7. To set the MMS importance or to request a read or delivery receipt, press Menu, and choose Options.

8. Modify the options.

9. Press Escape, and choose Save to save the changes.

10. Before you send the MMS, if you decide you need to move some things around in the body of the MMS—for example, you would rather have the text after the picture—put the cursor on the part or field you want to move, press Menu, and choose Move Field.

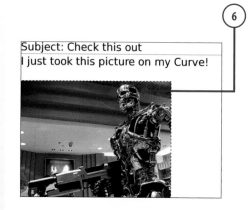

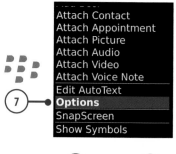

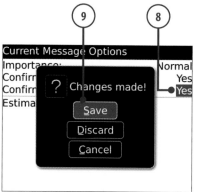

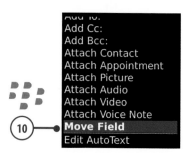

11. The field shows up and down arrows. Use the trackball or track-pad to scroll up and down to move that field up and down the message. Click the trackball or trackpad to select where to leave the field.

12. To send the MMS, click the trackball or trackpad, and choose Send.

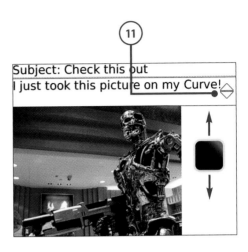

>>>step-by-step

Sending Multimedia Messages Directly

A quicker way to send MMS messages is directly from the file itself. This saves you from first composing an MMS and then attaching files.

1. Find the file you want to send via MMS. The file must be a picture, audio, video, or voice note. Press Menu, and choose Send As MMS.

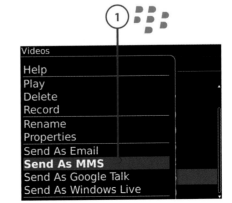

No Send as MMS Option

If you do not see Send as MMS, the file is too large.

---

2. Select one or more recipients from the address book.

3. If one of the recipients has a mobile number and one or more email addresses, the BlackBerry asks you to choose. If you know that the person cannot receive email on his phone, be sure you choose the phone number.

4. To send the MMS, click the trackball or trackpad, and choose Send.

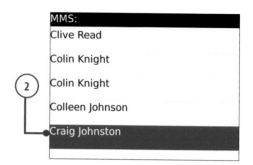

>>>step-by-step

Receiving and Replying to Multimedia Messages

Once you start sending MMS messages, you should start receiving them, too. As with all other messages, MMS messages are listed in the Messages application allowing you to open and reply to them.

1. When you receive a Multimedia Message, it will be listed in the message list. Notice that it has its own unique icon.

2. Click the message to open it.

3. If you want to save one of the pictures or videos in the MMS, scroll over the one you want to save so that it has a blue outline. For example, to save an image in an MMS, select it, press Menu, and choose Save image.

4. You can then browse your BlackBerry's memory or external media card for a place to save the image. It is a good idea to rename the image before you save it.

5. To reply to an MMS, click the trackball or trackpad, and choose Reply. You can also choose Reply to All or Forward.

6. When you type your reply you notice that the attachments are no longer visible, and the original MMS is now plain text. To send the reply, click the trackball or trackpad, and choose Send. Forwarding an MMS retains the attachments.

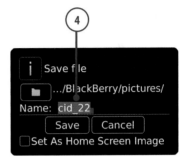

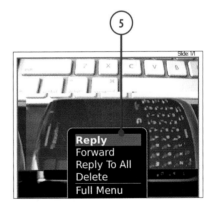

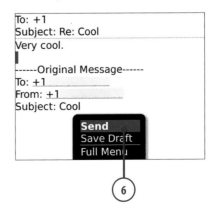

BlackBerry PIN Messages

Each BlackBerry has a hard-coded number, which is called its PIN. If you know someone's BlackBerry PIN, you can send messages directly to him or her. The benefit of sending a PIN message rather than to an email is that the path of the message is much shorter.

PIN Versus Email Paths

A regular email takes this path:

Sender's BlackBerry <-> Wireless Carrier <-> RIM NOC <-> BIS/BES <-> Email server <-> Recipient's email server <-> BIS/BES <-> RIM NOC <-> Wireless Carrier <-> Recipient's BlackBerry

A PIN message takes this path:

Sender's BlackBerry <-> Wireless Carrier <-> RIM NOC <-> Wireless Carrier <-> Recipient's BlackBerry.

PIN messages arrive almost instantly on the recipient's BlackBerry and are much quicker than regular emails, SMSs, and MMSs.

The BlackBerry PIN enables a common bond between BlackBerry users around the world because they share this unique ability. BlackBerry PIN to PIN messages, as they are called, can be sent from any BlackBerry to any BlackBerry in the world, no matter which wireless carrier is used.

To find your BlackBerry PIN, press Alt, Shift, and H at the same time.

>>>*step-by-step*

Sending a PIN Message

Now that you know what a BlackBerry PIN is and how to find your PIN, you are ready to send your first PIN message.

1. To compose a PIN message, from the Messages application, press Menu, and choose Compose PIN.

2. Start typing in the name of the person you want to PIN.

3. If you do not have the PIN entered for the recipient in the address book, you see a window pop up informing you of this.

   You can also just type in the recipients PIN into the To field.

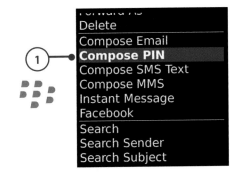

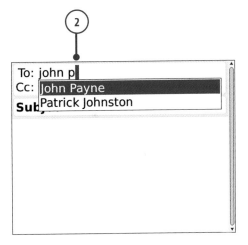

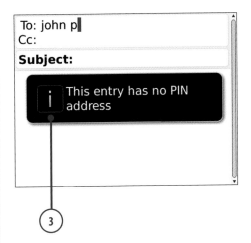

4. You can attach a vCard to a PIN message if you want to. To do this, press Menu, and choose Attach Contact.

5. To send the PIN message, click the trackball or trackpad, and choose Send.

6. When a PIN message has been sent, it is listed in the message list. After it has been delivered, the Sent icon includes a small D. Notice that PIN messages are the color red.

Delivered or Read?

Even though the D shows that a PIN message has been delivered, it does not mean that the PIN message has been read.

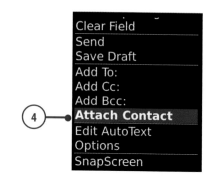

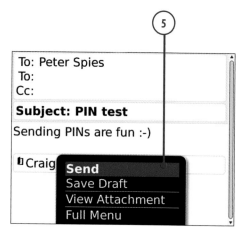

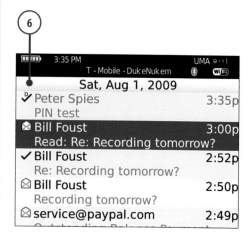

7. When you receive a new PIN message, it is listed in the message list in red and bold.

8. Click the trackball or trackpad to open the PIN message.

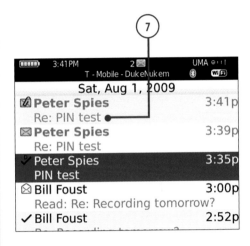

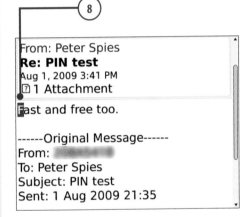

In this chapter, you learn about your BlackBerry Curve's calendar. The calendar keeps track of your life for you and reminds you where to be and when. You also learn about the date and time and how to keep that synchronized. Topics include the following:

8

→ Wireless and nonwireless calendar synchronization
→ Configuring the Calendar application
→ Creating and accepting appointments
→ Setting the time zone, date, and time

Working with Date and Time and the Calendar

Your BlackBerry Curve has a fully functioning calendar. You can use this calendar to schedule meetings, accept invitations to meetings, and even to look up someone's availability if you have a corporate BlackBerry on a BES.

In addition to the calendar, your BlackBerry Curve keeps perfect time because it can update its time from the BlackBerry clock (operated by RIM) or your wireless carrier's network time. Your BlackBerry Curve is also well aware of time zones, so it can be used anywhere in the world.

Configuring Time, Date, and Calendar

Before we work on the calendar, you need to ensure that your time and date are correct and that you use the correct time zone.

>>>*step-by-step*

Configuring Time and Date

All BlackBerry Curves support time zones, daylight savings time, and automatic time synchronization. Here is how to ensure your BlackBerry Curve is always on the right time.

1. From the BlackBerry Home Screen, click the Settings icon.

2. From the Settings folder, click the Options icon.

3. From the Settings screen, click Date/Time.

Time Seems Wrong

The network time does not reflect daylight savings time differences. So, if you are in daylight savings time where the time is artificially set back by one hour, the network time continues to reflect the real time. This is normal.

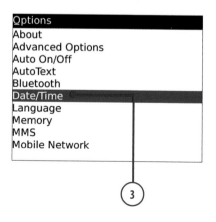

4. Verify that you have the correct Time Zone selected. Click the name of the time zone to see the full list.

5. After you select the correct time zone, ensure that the time is correct. Change it if necessary.

6. Select to display the time in 12-hour or 24-hour format.

7. Ensure the date is correct and correct it if necessary.

8. Select whether you want your BlackBerry Curve to synchronize the time automatically. You can choose to synchronize time with the wireless network (Network) or BlackBerry time (BlackBerry).

9. Network Time shows the actual network time.

10. Network Date reflects the actual date.

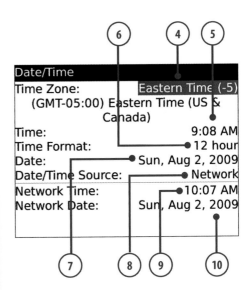

Date Seems Wrong

If you are in daylight savings time and it is just before midnight, the network time will be 1 hour ahead, so the date reflects the next day. This is normal.

11. When you have your date and time set correctly, press the Escape key, and choose Save to save your settings.

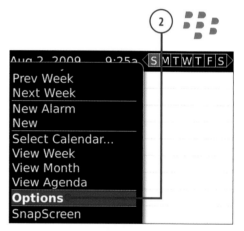

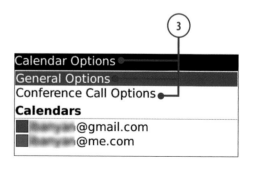

>>>step-by-step

Configuring the Calendar

Now that your BlackBerry is set to the correct date and time, you are ready to use your calendar. Before you add any new appointments, you might want to configure the Calendar the way you want it.

1. To open the Calendar application, click the Calendar icon on the BlackBerry Home Screen.

2. Click the Menu key, and choose Options.

3. The Calendar Options screen shows General Options, Conference Call Options, and options specific to the calendars you synchronize on your BlackBerry Curve. If your BlackBerry Curve is running OS 4.5 or lower, you cannot see the Conference Call options listed.

4. If you have a corporate BlackBerry, you can see your corporate calendar account listed as Desktop.

5. Click General Options.

6. Set the day that is the first day of your week. This is typically Sunday but might differ where you live.

7. Set the time of day you start your day.

8. Set the time of day you end your day.

9. Under View, set the Initial View. Your choices are Day, Week, Month, and Agenda. This view can be changed while using the Calendar application.

10. Show Free Time in Agenda View controls whether the Agenda View displays items that day in Free Time. If you set this to No, you only see appointments listed with no indication of when you are free.

11. Show End Time in Agenda View controls whether the Agenda View displays the end time for each appointment. If you set this to No, each appointment will be listed but only the start time will appear.

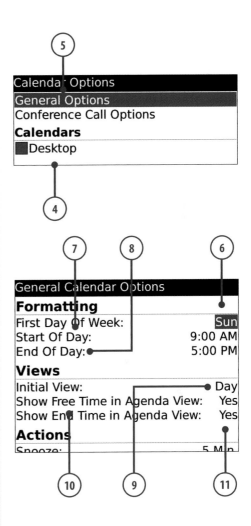

Quick Entry Explained

This is very useful when you just need to add an appointment without any participants. If you set this to No, the BlackBerry Curve assumes your keystrokes are commands (discussed a little later) instead of an appointment title.

12. Snooze enables you to set the default Snooze time in minutes. This setting controls the number of minutes that Snooze lasts.

13. Default Reminder enables you to set the default number of minutes a meeting reminder pops up before the actual start of the meeting.

14. Enable Quick Entry enables you to start typing a new appointment title while viewing the calendar.

15. Confirm Delete controls whether the BlackBerry Curve prompts you to confirm you actually want to delete an appointment.

16. Keep Appointments controls how long the BlackBerry keeps appointments after they occur. This can be set to 15 Days, 30 Days, 60 Days, 90 Days, and Forever.

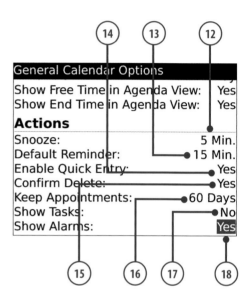

No Calendar Entries Deleted

This setting does not affect those same calendar entries you have in your corporate calendar account. When the number of days is reached, the BlackBerry simply removes them without removing them from your corporate account because it is considered to be a maintenance event.

17. Show Tasks controls whether the BlackBerry Curve includes Tasks in its views.

18. Show Alarms controls whether Alarms that you set display in the Calendar views.

Not Including Tasks

You can enter tasks using the Tasks application that is separate from the Calendar. Including tasks might be useful because they are almost always time sensitive.

Conference Call Options

Conference Call Options is visible only if your BlackBerry Curve runs OS 4.6 or later. This is useful if you have your own conference call bridge and need to include the bridge details in some meetings.

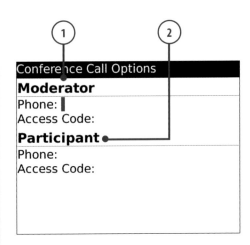

1. Under the Moderator section, you can enter the phone number to be called and the access code that the moderator must use to take control of the conference call.

2. Under the Participant section, you can enter the phone number to be called (which is typically the same number) and the access code that the participant must use to join the conference call.

3. For personal calendars, click the email address.

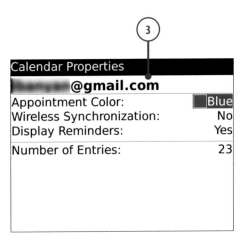

Corporate Versus Personal Calendars

On the Calendar Options screen under the Calendars heading, you see a list of your calendars. If you have a corporate BlackBerry, you should see your corporate calendar listed as the Desktop. If your BlackBerry is a personal device or if your company enables personal email accounts on your corporate BlackBerry, you see the different calendars listed by the email account's email address.

4. For corporate calendars, click Desktop.

5. Appointment Color enables you to set the color of each calendar's appointments.

Why Use Colors?

By default the BlackBerry Curve shows all calendars on the screen at the same time, so having appointments in different colors enables you to differentiate between calendars or corporate and personal appointments.

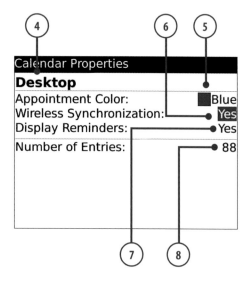

6. Wireless Synchronization works only for corporate calendars, and controls whether your BlackBerry synchronizes the calendar wirelessly between the device and your corporate calendar.

7. Display Reminders controls whether the BlackBerry displays reminders. Remember that these are settings for a particular calendar, so you might not want reminders for personal appointments, but only for corporate appointments.

8. Number of Entries is a display only field that displays how many calendar entries are in that particular calendar.

Navigating the Calendar

The Calendar application can display a number of different views:

- Day

Aug 2, 2009	9:29a ‹S M T W T F S›
9:00a	
10:00a	
11:00a	
12:00p	
1:00p	
2:00p	
3:00p	
4:00p	
5:00p	

- Week

Aug 2, 2009				Week 31			9:30a
Aug 2009	Sun 2	Mon 3	Tue 4	Wed 5	Thu 6	Fri 7	Sat 8
9:00a							
10:00a							
11:00a							
12:00p							
1:00p							
2:00p							
3:00p							
4:00p							
5:00p							

- Month

Aug 2, 2009			Week 31		9:30a	
August						
S	M	T	W	T	F	S
26	27	28	29	30	31	1
2	3	4	5	6	7	8
9	10	11	12	13	14	15
16	17	18	19	20	21	22
23	24	25	26	27	28	29
30	31	1	2	3	4	5

- Agenda

Aug 2, 2009	9:30a
Sun, Aug 2, 2009	
9:00a - 5:00p Free Time	
Mon, Aug 3, 2009	
9:00a - 5:00p Free Time	
Tue, Aug 4, 2009	
9:00a - 5:00p Free Time	

>>>*step-by-step*

Changing Calendar Views

You can change those views in two ways:

1. If you have the Enable Quick Entry set to No as we previously discussed, you can press D for Day View, W for Week View, M for Month View, or A for Agenda View.

2. If you have the Enable Quick Entry set to Yes, you can press Menu, and choose the view you want to switch to.

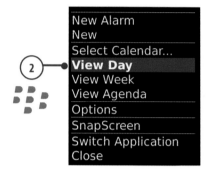

>>>*step-by-step*

Selecting the Calendar

By default, the Calendar application shows all calendars in the same view. If you have more than one calendar, you might want to switch between calendars instead of having them all in one view.

1. Press Menu, and choose Select Calendar.

2. Select your calendar, or choose to Show All Calendars.

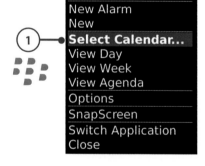

Using the Calendar

Now that you know how to navigate the calendar and configure it, let's find out how to send and accept appointments.

Use Quick Entry

If the appointment is just for you and you have the Enable Quick Entry set to Yes, just start typing the subject of the meeting and press Enter. The appointment is created instantly.

>>>*step-by-step*

Creating and Sending an Appointment

You can create an appointment for yourself or invite others to be part of the appointment.

1. To create a new appointment, if you are in Week or Day View, scroll to the time you want your appointment to start and click the trackball or trackpad.

2. The New Appointment screen displays.

3. Ensure that you create the appointment using the correct calendar by selecting it in the Send Using field.

4. Type a subject for the appointment.

5. Type a location for the appointment.

6. If the appointment is an all day event, check the All Day Event box.

7. Change the start and end date and time for the appointment. Appointments can span multiple days.

Duration Is Automatic

As you change the start and end dates and times, the Duration field changes to reflect the length of the appointment.

---

8. If you want to adjust the length of the appointment, modify the Duration field. When you make adjustments to this field, the end date and time of your meeting change.

9. Choose the time zone for the meeting.

Time Zones Are Important

If you travel to different time zones, ensure that you select the correct time zone for the meeting so that when you are in that time zone, the meeting reflects the correct date and time.

---

10. Change the Show Time As field to reflect how your time needs to be represented during that appointment. Your choices are Free, Tentative, Busy, and Out of Office. This is very useful in a corporate environment.

11. Change the Reminder if you need to.

12. If you host a conference call, check the Conference Call box. If you previously set up the Conference Call settings, those values will be inserted into the meeting. If not, you can type them in now.

13. If the appointment recurs, click to set it to Daily, Weekly, Monthly, or Yearly.

Recurrence Is Intelligent

If you choose anything other than None, you see more options to set up that recurring appointment. For example, for daily recurring appointments you can choose the frequency and ending date. For weekly recurring meetings, you can select the day of the week they occur on, the frequency, and when they end.

---

14. If this appointment is private, check the Mark as Private box.

15. Enter any notes for this appointment.

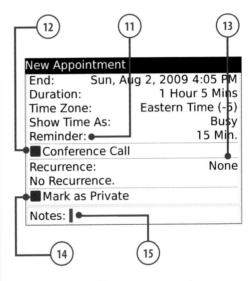

Daily recurrence options

Weekly recurrence options

16. If you want to invite others to the appointment, press Menu, and choose Invite Attendee.

17. You can choose people from your BlackBerry Address Book. If you use a corporate BlackBerry, you can perform a Lookup to find coworkers.

18. If you use a corporate BlackBerry, you see an extra button called View Availability.

Free/Busy Lookup

This enables you to see when your invitees are available. The BlackBerry checks their calendars and displays their availability on the screen. You can scroll left and right to select a more appropriate time slot when everyone is free.

19. To save your appointment and send out invitations to your appointment if you added attendees, press Escape, and choose Save.

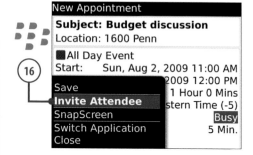

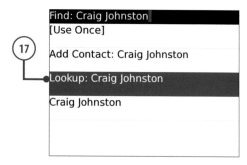

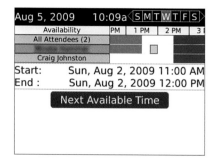

Receiving and Responding to Appointments

When someone invites you to an appointment or meeting, you receive that request on your BlackBerry Curve. You can then act upon it.

1. When you receive a meeting request, it arrives in your messages list. The icon for the meeting request looks different from the emails and other types of messages.

2. When you click the meeting request, you see the details of that request.

Conflicts

If the meeting conflicts with another one in your calendar or it is adjacent to another meeting in your calendar, you are warned.

---

3. When you are ready to respond, click the trackball or trackpad, and choose how to respond.

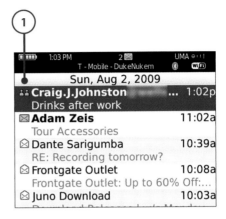

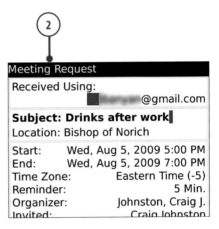

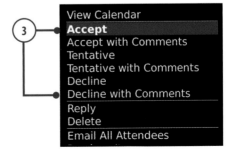

4. If you choose to respond with comments, you are taken to a screen to type those. After you have typed your comments, click the trackball or trackpad, and choose Send.

5. The meeting request response replaces the meeting request in your message list.

6. If you go back to the Calendar application, you see the appointment you accepted.

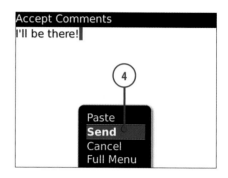

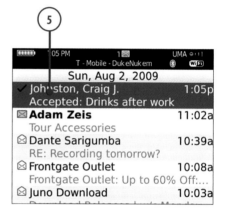

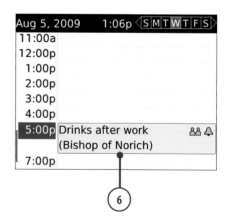

Configuring Alarms

In addition to appointments, you can set alarms. These alarms are separate from the daily alarms that you can set in the Clock application, which we cover next.

1. To create a new alarm, press Menu, and choose New Alarm.

2. Type in the subject of the alarm.

3. Change the date and time of the alarm.

4. Choose whether the alarm is a one time alarm or a recurring alarm.

5. If you choose a recurring alarm, extra options appear to enable you to configure the recurring information.

6. To save the alarm, press Escape, and choose Save.

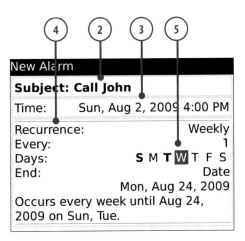

Show Alarm in Calendar

The alarm doesn't display in your calendar unless you set Show Alarms to Yes in the General Calendar Options.

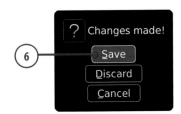

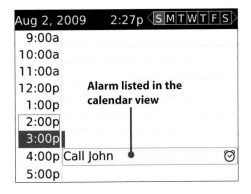

Alarm listed in the calendar view

Synchronizing the Calendar with a PC and Mac

If you don't have a corporate BlackBerry and do not use a wireless synchronization program such as Google Sync, you can synchronize your BlackBerry with a PC or Mac.

>>>step-by-step

Synchronize with Windows

To synchronize your BlackBerry Curve with Windows, you need to install the BlackBerry Desktop Manager. If you have not yet done this, please take a few minutes to follow the instructions in the Prologue.

1. Run Desktop Manager and connect your BlackBerry Curve using its USB cable.

2. Click Synchronize.

3. When in the Synchronize screen, click Synchronization.

4. Click the Synchronization button.

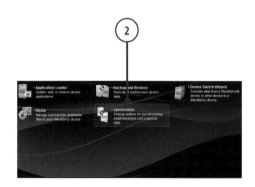

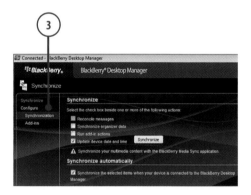

5. When the Intellisync screen opens, check the box next to Calendar.

6. On the Calendar Setup screen, choose the desktop application to synchronize your BlackBerry Curve with.

Can I Use My Calendar Program?

This list depends on the applications you installed on your computer. For example, if you have Outlook installed, it is listed here.

7. Choose the type of synchronization.

8. The next screen shows the Calendar date range options. If you chose Yahoo!, you can click the Options button to type in your Yahoo! Username and password. Other calendar applications like Outlook will not require a password.

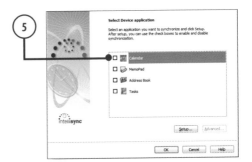

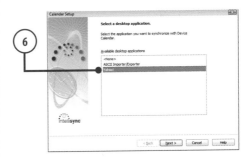

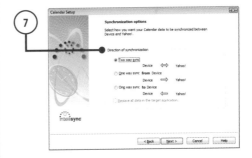

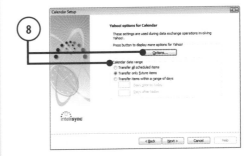

9. After you click Next, you see the Congratulations screen, and when you click Finish, you return to the Intellisync screen.

10. If you want to further configure the Calendar synchronization settings, ensure that Calendar is selected, and click the Advanced button.

11. The Advanced Calendar screen shows five sections: Folder Mapping, Confirmations, Conflict Resolution, Filters, and Field Mapping.

12. Folder Mapping is not used in Calendar synchronization.

13. Confirmations enables you to choose when to receive confirmations in Windows when synchronization occurs.

14. If you click the Conflict Resolution button, you can set up how Intellisync handles conflicts between the BlackBerry and the desktop calendar program.

Note

If you are doing two-way synching, conflicts can occur between the BlackBerry and the desktop program. For example, if a particular calendar item is changed in both places. You choices are

- **Add All Conflicting Items.** This creates duplicate copies of a conflicting item enabling you to rectify the conflict after the fact.

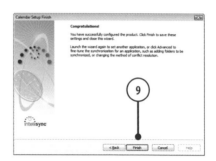

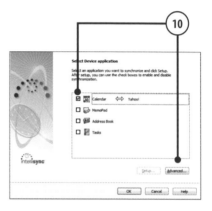

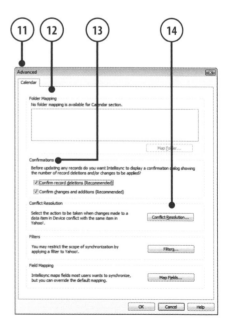

- **Ignore All Conflicting Items**. This simply ignores any conflicts.

- **Notify Me When Conflicts Occur**. This tells Intellisync to pop up a dialog box indicating when a conflict occurs and enables you to resolve it in real time.

- **Device Wins**. This means that if there is a conflict, the version of the item on the BlackBerry always wins, and the item in the desktop application will be ignored.

- **Server Wins (in this case Yahoo! Wins)**. This means that if a conflict occurs, the version of the item in the desktop application (or in this case Yahoo!) wins and the item on the BlackBerry will be ignored.

15. If you click the Filters button, you can create filters that filter out certain appointments.

16. To create a new filter, click New.

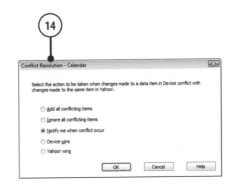

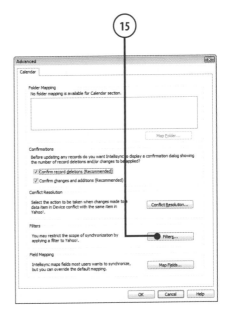

17. Type in a filter name.

18. Select a field, operator, and value to create a new condition. For example, filter appointments where the Subject contains the word Testing. Click Add to List to add the condition to the filter.

19. If you have multiple conditions in a filter, click the Rules tab to set whether all conditions must be met, or just some of them.

20. Click the Map Fields button if you need to change the mappings of fields in the desktop application to the ones on the BlackBerry.

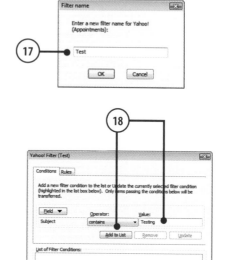

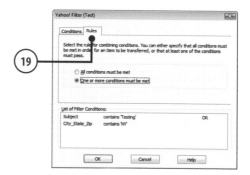

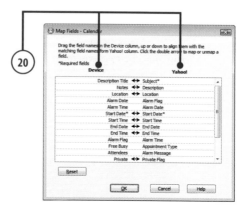

21. Back on the main Intellisync screen, click OK to save your changes. These calendar synchronization options are used each time you connect your BlackBerry to your computer.

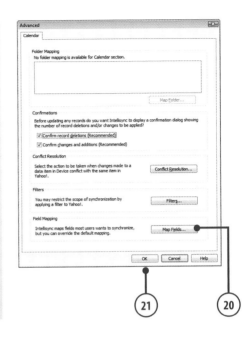

Synchronize with a Mac

You can use two programs to synchronize calendars with your Mac: PocketMac for BlackBerry and Missing Sync for BlackBerry.

If you haven't already installed one of these applications on your Mac, take a few minutes to follow the instructions in the Prologue.

BlackBerry Desktop Manager for Mac OS X

After the writing of this book, RIM released BlackBerry Desktop Manager for Mac OS X. There was no time to include it in the book, but you can read an online article that covers this new application in detail: www.MyBlackBerryCurve.info.

1. Run Pocketmac for BlackBerry, and connect your BlackBerry Curve using the USB cable.

2. Click the picture of the BlackBerry to set up PocketMac for your BlackBerry.

3. Click the Calendar tab.

4. Put a check mark next to Sync Calendar between the BlackBerry and Mac.

5. Put a check mark next to the application you want to synchronize with.

6. Click the Advanced Preferences button to the right of that application.

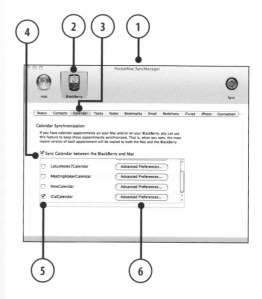

7. The first two radio buttons enable you to configure which calendar categories to synchronize. The categories on the BlackBerry translate into calendars on the Mac.

8. The Default for mobile-device-created items enables you to set which calendar category items created on your BlackBerry will synchronize to on your Mac.

9. The last three radio buttons enable you to configure the type of synchronization:

- Two-way sync is when calendar items on your Mac are sent to your BlackBerry and items on your BlackBerry are sent to your Mac.

- Overwrite device is a one-way synchronization where the calendar items on your Mac overwrite ones on your BlackBerry.

- Overwrite Mac is a one-way synchronization where the calendar items on your BlackBerry overwrite ones on your Mac.

10. If you want to limit how far back the appointments go, check the box labeled Ignore appointments older than, and type in a number of days.

11. Click Save to save your changes.

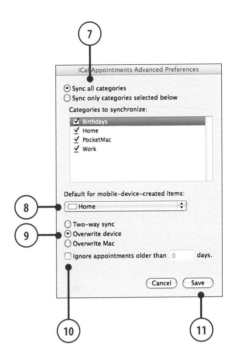

>>>step-by-step

Missing Sync for BlackBerry

Remember that after the first time you synchronize your BlackBerry with Missing Sync for BlackBerry through the USB cable, you can do all future syncs using Bluetooth. This means that when your BlackBerry comes within range of your Mac, it synchronizes.

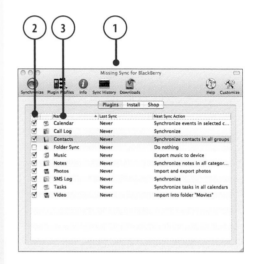

1. Connect your BlackBerry to your Mac using the USB cable, and run Missing Sync for BlackBerry.

2. On the main screen, put a check mark next to Calendar.

3. Double-click Calendar to change the settings.

4. Under Calendar Settings, choose the type of synchronization that occurs:

   • Synchronize is a two-way synchronization.

   • Overwrite device with desktop data on next sync only tells Missing Sync to overwrite all data on the BlackBerry the next time it synchronizes but to return to the previous method of synchronization after that.

   • Always overwrite device with desktop data tells Missing Sync to always overwrite the calendar data on your BlackBerry with the data on the Mac.

5. Under Synchronize, you can choose to synchronize all Mac calendars with the BlackBerry or just the selected ones. Calendars on the Mac translate into Calendar categories on your BlackBerry.

6. Put events created on the device into tells Missing Sync that any appointments created on the BlackBerry must be synchronized to a particular calendar on the Mac. The default is Home.

7. The Sync setting enables you to control how far back in time and how far forward in time to synchronize calendar items.

8. Click OK to save your changes.

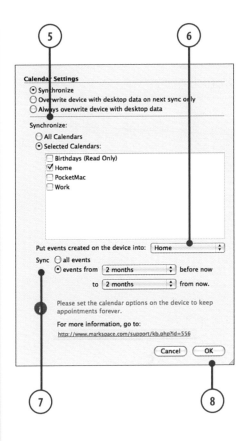

>>>step-by-step

The Clock Application

If your BlackBerry Curve runs OS 4.6 or higher, you have a Clock application that includes the Alarm functionality which was previously a separate application on older BlackBerry Curves. It adds a large clock face, Timer, and Stopwatch. You can also use the clock as a bedside clock.

1. To run the Clock application, click the Clock icon on the BlackBerry Home Screen.

2. The main clock screen appears. The majority of the screen is taken up with a clock whereas the bottom portion of the screen displays any alarms that you set.

Different Types of Alarms

The alarms displayed include the daily alarm you set plus any alarms you might have set in the Calendar application.

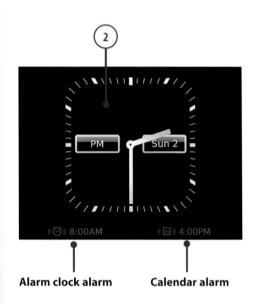

Alarm clock alarm   **Calendar alarm**

>>>*step-by-step*

Configuring the Clock Application

The Clock application is surprisingly flexible and has many options that you can use to personalize it.

1. To configure the clock application, press Menu, and choose Options.

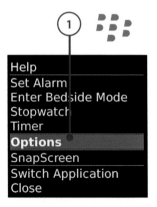

2. The clock options appear. Under the Clock heading, you can change the Clock Face. Besides the default of Analog, your choices are:

- Digital

- Flip Clock

- LCD Digital

3. Home Time Zone enables you to set your home time zone, which might be different from the time zone you are in.

Home Time Explained
Selecting a home time zone that differs from the primary system time zone displays a second clock for the specified home time zone. The home time zone time is indicated by a little house icon. You can display time in New York and in London on the clock application.

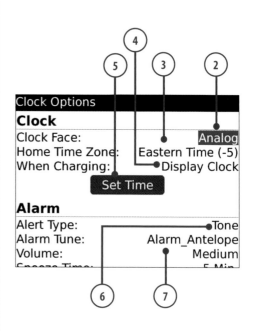

4. When Charging enables you to set what the BlackBerry Curve must do when you plug it in to charge. Your options are Do Nothing, Display Clock, and Enter Bedside Mode.

5. If you click the Set Time button, you go to the BlackBerry's main Date/Time options screen.

6. Under the Alarm heading, you can change how the alarm sounds. You can change Alarm Type to Tone, Vibrate, or Tone+vibrate.

7. You can change Alarm Tune so that something different plays when the alarm sounds.

Changing Alarm Tune
Click the name of the sound to see a list of all installed sounds. Scroll to the top of the list, and click Browse to see any sounds you might have installed yourself, or select music.

8. Volume controls how loud the tune plays. The options are Low, Medium, High, Escalating. When set to Escalating the alarm sounds start off soft and get progressively louder until it is silenced.

9. Snooze Time controls how long the alarm must snooze for when you click snooze.

10. Number of Vibrations controls how many times your BlackBerry vibrates if it is set to vibrate when the alarm goes off. It can be set to 1, 2, or 3.

11. Disable LED controls whether to disable the notification LED when your BlackBerry enters Bedside Mode, which is designed to turn the clock into a bedside clock. This is useful to stop it from flashing and waking you up.

12. Disable Radio controls whether your BlackBerry disables its cellular radio when it enters Bedside Mode. This is useful when trying to save on battery life.

13. Dim Screen controls whether your BlackBerry dims the screen when it enters Bedside Mode. It is useful to set this to Yes so that the screen doesn't keep you awake.

14. Under the Stopwatch heading there is one setting: Stopwatch Face. You can set this to Analog or Digital; this is for the Stopwatch functionality only.

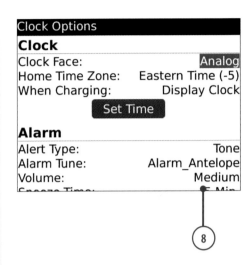

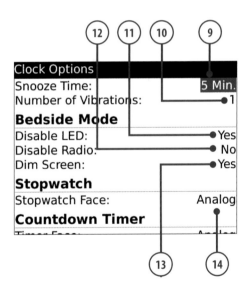

15. Under the Countdown Timer, settings control the functionality of the Timer. Timer Face controls whether the Timer has an Analog or Digital face. This is only for the Timer.

16. Timer Tune controls what tune plays when the Timer runs out.

17. Volume controls how loud the tune plays.

18. Vibrate controls whether the Timer should also vibrate when the timer expires.

Clock Options

Disable LED:	Yes
Disable Radio:	No
Dim Screen:	Yes

Stopwatch

Stopwatch Face:	Analog

Countdown Timer

Timer Face:	Analog
Timer Tune:	Timer_3beeps
Volume:	Medium
Vibrate	No

>>>step-by-step

Using the Clock

Now that the Clock application is set up, let's see how you can use it. As you saw from the options, it is a clock, alarm clock, stop watch, and timer.

1. To set the alarm, click the trackball or trackpad and the alarm time appears.

2. Use the trackball or trackpad to scroll through the time.

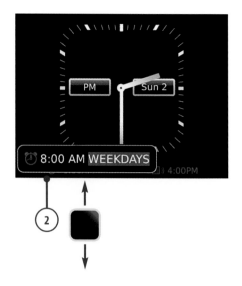

Setting the Alarm

To the right of the alarm time, you can set when the alarm sounds. Set this to On, Off, or Weekdays. Weekdays is particularly useful for when you need to wake up during a work week but not on the weekends.

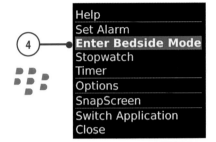

3. Click the trackball or trackpad to save the alarm settings.

4. To enter Bedside Mode manually, press Menu, and choose Enter Bedside Mode.

5. To start the Timer function, press Menu, and choose Timer.

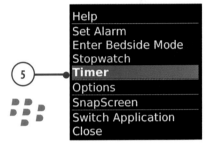

6. To set the Timer, press Menu, and choose Set Timer.

7. Use the trackball or trackpad to change the amount of time the Timer needs to countdown. Click Start to start the Timer.

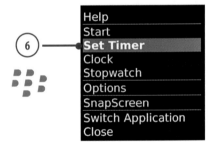

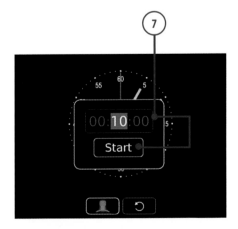

8. To use the Stopwatch, press Menu, and choose Stopwatch.

9. Press the green start/stop button to start and stop the Stopwatch or the reset icon to reset the Stopwatch.

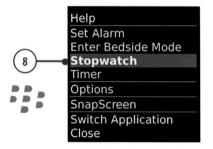

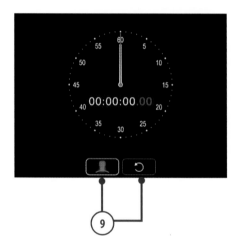

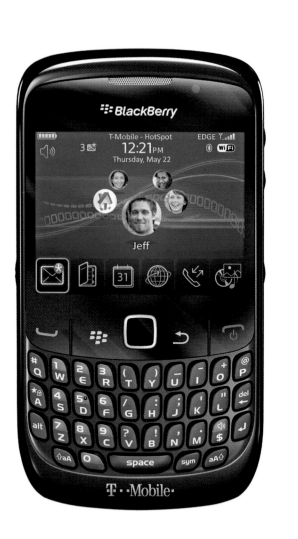

In this chapter, you learn about how to find, install, and use BlackBerry applications. Applications are what make a smartphone such as the BlackBerry Curve so useful and fun to use. Topics include the following:

→ BlackBerry App World
→ Installing applications not found on BlackBerry App World
→ Desktop install versus Over The Air install
→ Application permissions

Working with BlackBerry Applications

When you purchase your BlackBerry Curve, it has many built-in applications that make it useful and fun to use; however, you can choose from thousands of third-party applications that other people have developed for the BlackBerry Curve. Many of these applications are available through the BlackBerry App World, and many others are available through other online software websites such as Handandgo.

Applications written for the BlackBerry have been around since the BlackBerry first started addicting us to smartphones back in 1999, but it is more recently that RIM has created the BlackBerry App World. This is a central location for all BlackBerry applications. You can purchase these applications or download them for free right on your BlackBerry. This approach makes them very accessible and easy to find.

BlackBerry App World

BlackBerry App World is RIM's official application store for the BlackBerry. Developers can submit their applications to the store and either offer them for free, or charge a small fee. You can download these applications or purchase them using your PayPal account. BlackBerry App World will even notify you when an upgrade to that application is available.

>>>*step-by-step*

Installing BlackBerry App World

Your BlackBerry Curve might already have BlackBerry App World pre-installed; if not you can install it over the air.

1. Go to www.blackberry.com/appworld/download in the BlackBerry Browser.

2. Click Download.

3. Select your language, and click Next.

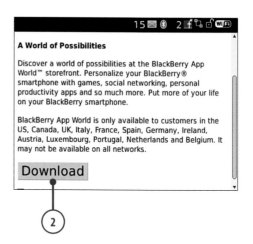

4. Click Download on the application details screen.

5. After BlackBerry App World downloads, you are prompted to reboot. You must do so to complete the install before trying to use BlackBerry App World.

6. When BlackBerry App World is installed, run it by clicking Downloads from the BlackBerry Home Screen. If you use a BlackBerry Curve with an OS lower than 4.6, you can see the BlackBerry App World icon on the Home Screen.

4

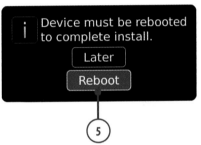

5

6

7. From the Downloads folder, click BlackBerry App World.

8. Scroll to the bottom of the incredibly long End User License Agreement, and click I Accept.

9. The main BlackBerry App World screen is dominated by the Featured applications. You can scroll left and right with the trackball or trackpad to see all the Featured applications.

   On the bottom of the screen, you can find more icons.

10. If you click Categories, you see the available applications grouped by category.

11. If you click Top Free, you see a list of the top 25 free applications.

12. If you click Top Paid, you see a list of the top 25 paid applications.

13. If you click Search, you can search for applications based on key words.

14. If you click My World, you can log in to your PayPal account to see a list of previously installed applications.

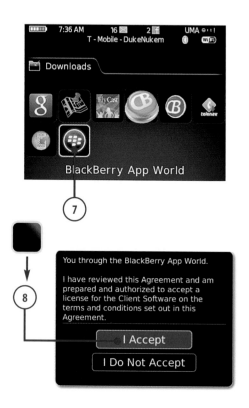

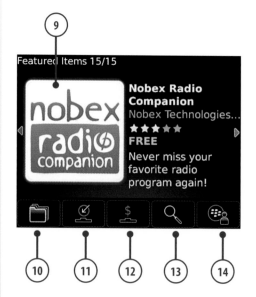

>>>*step-by-step*

Creating a PayPal Account

To purchase applications using the BlackBerry App World, you need a PayPal account. PayPal is a service that enables you to purchase items online using just your email address. Others can send money to you using just your email address. Before you continue, you must create a PayPal account if you don't already have one.

1. To sign up for a PayPal account, browse to http://www.PayPal.com. Click Sign Up.

2. On the next screen, choose the type of PayPal account you want. You need a Personal account only to use BlackBerry App World.

3. Enter your information, and click Agree and Create Account.

4. When your account has been created, you need to add a bank account or credit card to your PayPal account so that you can make purchases online and in BlackBerry App World.

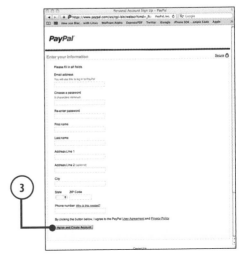

>>>step-by-step

My World

When your PayPal account has been completely set up, you are ready to use BlackBerry App World.

1. Click My World.

2. Press Menu, and choose Log In.

3. Type in your PayPal email address and password, and click Log In.

My World Explained

After you log in to My World using your PayPal email address and password, you see the My World screen. This screen lists any applications that you have downloaded or purchased through BlackBerry App World. If there are any updates to one of those applications, that will be indicated and you can simply click the update to install it.

Categories

Let's look at Categories next. All applications are given a category and if you know you need an application from a specific category but have no preference on the application name, this is a good place to start.

1. The Categories icon groups applications by category.

2. Many categories have subcategories. For example, if you click the Games category, you will be presented with different genres of games.

3. Clicking a subcategory reveals all the games in the subcategory along with a search bar at the top of the screen.

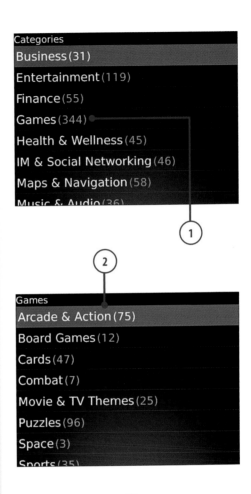

4. If you click the icon to the right of the search field, you can sort the list of applications. The list can be sorted by Popular, Newest, Rating, Price, Vendor, and App Name.

5. When you enter text into the search bar at the top of the screen, the list of applications sorts in real time based on what you type. The list includes applications that include the word you type in the title or vendor fields.

6. To buy an application or download one (if it is free), click the application.

Application Details

You see a screen showing more information about that application. The top half of the screen shows the application name, vendor, and rating. It also shows the price (or FREE if it is free) and how much memory that application takes up on your BlackBerry. There is also a Download button. If the application is not free, the Download button becomes a Purchase button.

7. If you scroll down a bit, you see a Reviews button. If you click this, you can read other BlackBerry user's reviews.

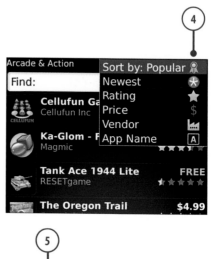

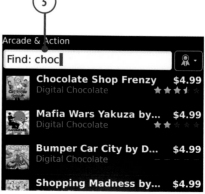

8. If you click Screenshots, you see one or more application screenshots.

9. If you keep scrolling, you can read the description of the application. At the bottom of the screen you see a Contact Support button. When you click this, you can send an email to the application vendor.

10. To download a free application, click Download.

11. The application starts download-ing immediately and installs automatically.

12. If an application is not free, the Download button becomes a Purchase button. To purchase the application, click Purchase.

13. You will be told that you need a PayPal account. Click OK.

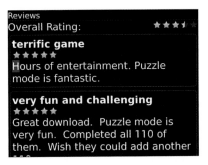

14. You then need to provide your PayPal password. After you type the password, click Login.

15. You see a summary of the purchase you are about to make. Click Buy Now.

16. The application automatically downloads and installs.

>>>*step-by-step*

Top Free and Top Paid

Applications that are available in the BlackBerry App World can be free or require a purchase. Top Free lists the top 25 free applications while Top Paid lists the top 25 paid applications.

1. Click the Top Free icon on the main BlackBerry App World screen. You see the top 25 free BlackBerry applications.

2. Click the Top Paid icon on the main BlackBerry App World screen. You see the top paid BlackBerry applications.

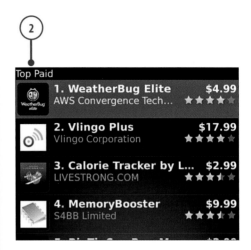

>>>step-by-step

Search

If you still haven't found the application you are looking for, try searching for it.

1. Click the Search icon on the main BlackBerry App World screen.

2. Type in a search term, and press Enter.

3. If you click the icon to the right of the search field, you can sort the search results. You can sort by Relevance, Newest, Rating, Price, Vendor, and App Name.

BlackBerry Applications Not in BlackBerry App World

If you are looking for a BlackBerry application and you cannot find it in the BlackBerry App World, you still have places you can look.

Other online stores sell BlackBerry applications. Handandgo.com, Pocketgear.com, Handmark.com, and CrackBerry.com—to name just a few. All these stores enable you to install the applications either Over the Air (OTA) or by downloading the application to your desktop computer and installing it using the USB cable.

Some of these online retailers also offer a special BlackBerry client similar to BlackBerry App World that enables you to browse their catalog right on your BlackBerry and download and purchase applications without the need for a desktop computer.

>>>step-by-step

Installing Applications Over the Air (OTA)

Many stores offer the ability to purchase and install BlackBerry applications Over the Air (OTA). After you purchase an application, the online store sends you either an SMS or an email containing a download link.

1. An email or SMS will arrive with a link to a JAD file.

What Is a JAD File?

JAD stands for Java Application Descriptor and is essentially a file that describes the Java application (in this case a BlackBerry application), the files that make up that application, and URLs to those files.

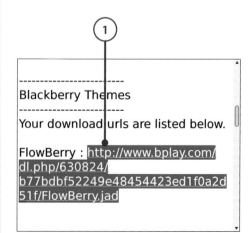

Blackberry Themes

Your download urls are listed below.

FlowBerry : http://www.bplay.com/dl.php/630824/b77bdbf52249e48454423ed1f0a2d51f/FlowBerry.jad

2. When you click the link, the BlackBerry Browser automatically loads up and connects to that link. You then see a description of the application including its name, version, vendor who created it, size, and description. The Description field sometimes contains special instructions.

3. When you click Download, the application downloads and installs.

Installing Applications Using a Computer

Another way that BlackBerry applications can be installed is with a computer. Online stores sometimes require you to download the BlackBerry application to your computer before installing it.

When you download a BlackBerry application to your computer, it is normally compressed into a ZIP file. When you uncompress the ZIP file, the application always contains a file ending in ALX. This is similar to the JAD file we previously discussed. Like the JAD file, the ALX file describes the application and points to the files that it contains. The files normally end in COD.

Installing Using an Apple Mac

First, we show you how to install BlackBerry software from your Mac using PocketMac for BlackBerry.

>>>*step-by-step*

1. Connect your BlackBerry to your Mac using the USB cable. Run PocketMac for BlackBerry.

2. Click the BlackBerry to see the configuration. Click the Utilities menu, and select Install Software to Device.

3. You can browse for the BlackBerry application. Remember that you must find the ALX file. When you find the ALX file, select it, and click Open.

4. You are then asked if you want to install that application. Click Yes.

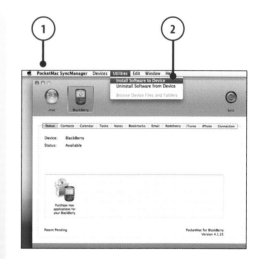

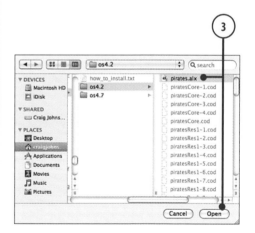

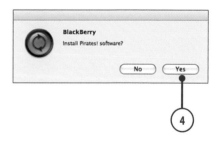

>>>step-by-step

Installing Using a Windows PC

Next we show you how to install BlackBerry software using your Windows PC.

As before, download the application to your PC, uncompress it, and be sure you know where the ALX file is.

1. Connect your BlackBerry Curve to your computer and run BlackBerry Desktop Manager. Click Application Loader.

2. On the next screen, click Start in the Add/Remove Applications section.

3. The BlackBerry Desktop Manager queries your device for a few seconds.

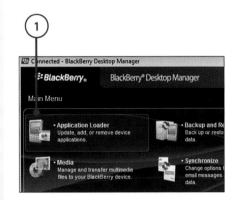

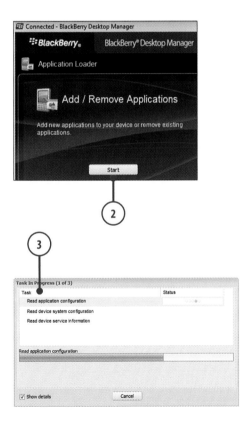

4. You then see a list of BlackBerry applications including the ones that make up the BlackBerry operating system. Click Browse.

5. Browse your hard drive and find the ALX file for the application you want to install. Select it, and click Open.

6. If you scroll down in the list of applications, you can see the new application listed with a check mark next to its name. The check mark signifies that it will be installed. Click Next.

7. You are shown a summary of the actions to be taken. You should see an action that says that Your BlackBerry Device Will Be Updated to Include the Following Software. Your new application should be listed there.

8. Click Finish to complete the install.

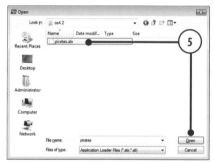

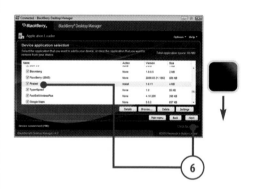

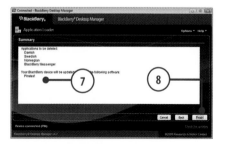

Deleting BlackBerry Applications

Sometimes you need to remove applications from your BlackBerry. Reasons can include the need to free up some memory, or an application that you don't use anymore.

Alternative Methods

If your BlackBerry Curve runs software lower than 4.6.0, you need to use your desktop computer to delete those applications or, on your BlackBerry, go to Options, Advanced Options, Applications. Scroll to an application, press Menu and choose Delete.

>>>*step-by-step*

Deleting Applications on the Device

There are two ways to delete BlackBerry applications. If your BlackBerry Curve is running software 4.6.0 or higher, you can delete most applications directly on your BlackBerry.

1. Select the application that you want to delete. Press Menu, and choose Delete.

2. An Are You Sure screen pops up. Click Delete.

1 Select the application to delete

2

Deleting Applications Using Your Desktop

If you use Windows, you need to use the BlackBerry Desktop Manager to select applications on your BlackBerry Curve. If you use a Mac you can use PocketMac for BlackBerry.

Here are the Windows steps.

1. Connect your BlackBerry Curve to your PC and run BlackBerry Desktop Manager. Click Application Loader.

2. On the next screen, click Start in the Add/Remove Applications section.

3. BlackBerry Desktop Manager now reads information from your device.

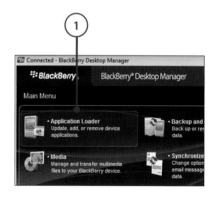

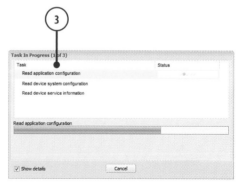

4. A check mark appears next to the applications that are installed. Find the application that you want to uninstall and uncheck the box next to that application. Click Next.

5. The Summary Screen shows the actions to be performed. Click Finish.

6. Next you see a screen showing the application's modules being removed from your BlackBerry Curve.

7. After all modules have been removed, your BlackBerry might reboot on its own. Do not disconnect it. Wait for the Update Complete screen to appear. When it appears, click Main Menu.

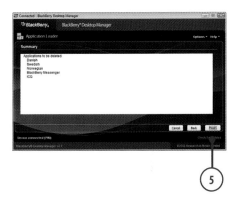

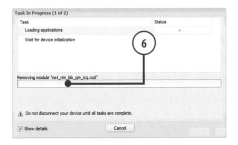

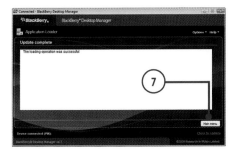

>>>*step-by-step*

Deleting Applications Using PocketMac for BlackBerry

Next, delete applications using PocketMac for BlackBerry.

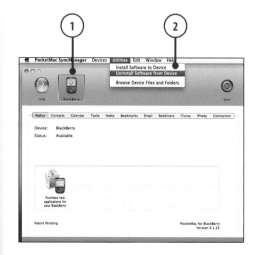

1. Connect your BlackBerry Curve to your Mac and run PocketMac for BlackBerry. Click the BlackBerry to see the configuration.

2. Click the Utilities menu and choose Uninstall Software from Device.

3. You see a screen listing all the applications that you previously installed using PocketMac for BlackBerry. Select the application that you want to uninstall and click Uninstall.

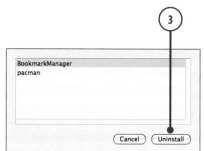

4. You see a confirmation screen. Click Yes and the selected software is removed from your BlackBerry. A reboot might be needed to complete the uninstallation process.

It's Not All Good

Unfortunately, PocketMac for BlackBerry uninstalls only applications that you installed on your BlackBerry Curve using PocketMac for BlackBerry. If you installed any software OTA and cannot remove it on the device, PocketMac for BlackBerry does not see those applications and therefore you cannot remove them.

Using BlackBerry Maps

The BlackBerry Curve is preinstalled with many applications that we have not covered. These include a Memo Pad, Tasks, Calculator, and games. One application however, is worth covering in more detail.

The BlackBerry Curve is preinstalled with an application called Maps. The Maps application uses your BlackBerry Curve's built-in GPS (or an external GPS if your BlackBerry Curve does not have GPS) to find places of interest or an address you type in.

BlackBerry Maps covers many regions of the world, but you should make sure your area is covered by visiting this link: http://na.blackberry.com/eng/devices/features/blackberry_maps.jsp#tab_tab_coverage.

>>>*step-by-step*

Loading BlackBerry Maps

Let's get started by loading BlackBerry Maps and getting ready to use it.

1. To run BlackBerry Maps, click the Maps icon. This icon might appear on the BlackBerry Home Screen or in the Applications folder.

2. You see a zoomed-out map.

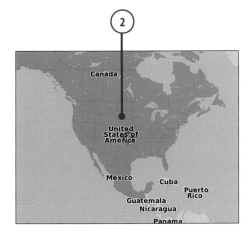

3. First, let's configure Maps. Press Menu, and choose Options. You see the Maps Options screen.

4. Under GPS Settings you can find GPS Source, which is the device that the BlackBerry must use for GPS coordinates.

5. Backlight Timeout When enables you to set when the backlight turns off. By default it is set to < 100% Battery, which means that if your BlackBerry's battery is not at 100%, the backlight turns off after the regular backlight timeout period.

Should I Adjust This?

This is useful when driving with your BlackBerry and you have it plugged in. This setting can be changed to < 75%, < 50%, and < 25%. Changing this setting is useful if you do not have your BlackBerry plugged in. The backlight turns off after the battery reaches 75%, 50%, or 25% power.

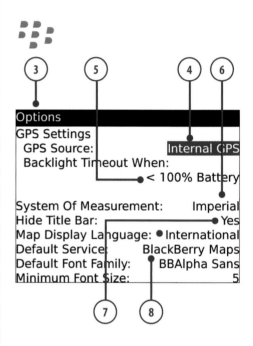

6. System Of Measurement configures the BlackBerry to display either Imperial or Metric measurements.

7. You can set Hide Title Bar to Yes or No, which enables you to hide the title bar that displays the battery power, time, signal strength, and any message indicators.

8. You cannot change the Default Service.

Which GPS Device?

If your BlackBerry has GPS built-in, you see Internal GPS. Leave it set to this. If your BlackBerry Curve does not have built-in GPS, you can click to see a list of external GPS devices that you have previously paired with via Bluetooth. If you have not paired with an external GPS puck or GPS mouse, follow the steps in Chapter 4, "Connecting: Internet, Bluetooth, and VPNs."

9. Default Font Family enables you to change the font used within the Maps application.

10. Minimum Font Size enables you to change the minimum font size used by the Maps application.

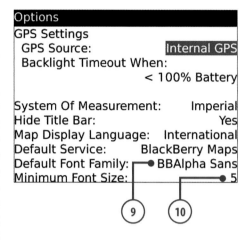

Find A Location

Use Maps to find a location.

1. Press Menu, and choose Find Location. You see a screen with a few Find options.

2. Click Where I Am to find your current location.

3. Click Enter Address to type in an address.

4. Click From Contacts to browse your BlackBerry address book. You can then select someone from the address book that has a physical address listed.

5. Click Recent to select recently used addresses.

6. Click Favorites to select from addresses you previously marked as favorites.

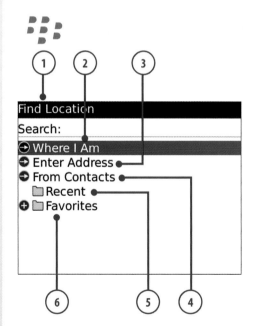

7. If you click Where I Am, Maps plots your location on the map.

8. To zoom into your location, press Menu, and choose Zoom to Point. This zooms into street level.

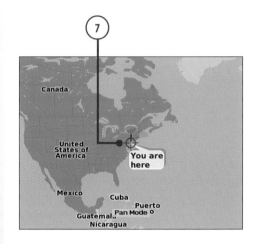

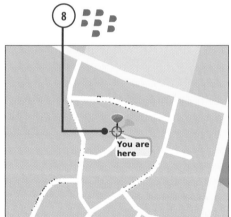

>>>*step-by-step*

Send Someone Your Location or Any Location

When you find a location, you can send it to someone.

1. Press Menu, and choose Send Location.

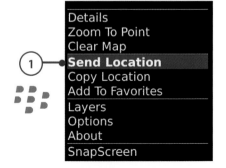

2. Select the method you want to
    use to send the location.

3. A URL to the location pastes into
    the message. All you need to do is
    address the message and send it.

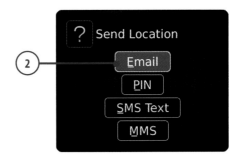

>>>step-by-step

Finding Places of Interest Around You

Let's say you have found your location on the map and need to find a
local pizza place.

1. Press Menu, and choose Local
    Search.

2. You can type any search terms
    into the Search field, such as cof-
    fee, pizza, restaurants, and so on.

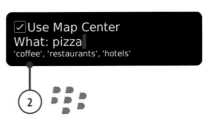

3. Your search results show places that match the key word you typed that are close to your location. To view those places on the map, click View On Map.

4. As you scroll over the phone number and click the trackball or trackpad, a dialog box pops up asking if you would like to call.

5. If you want to see the location on the map, scroll over the place's name, click the trackball or trackpad, and choose View On Map.

6. To get directions to this location, press Menu, and choose Get Directions.

7. The Get Directions screen displays. Presuming that you want to get directions to the pizza restaurant from your current location, click Where I Am.

8. To select the pizza restaurant you just found, look under From Map. You should see the place you just saw on the map. Click it to select the End Location.

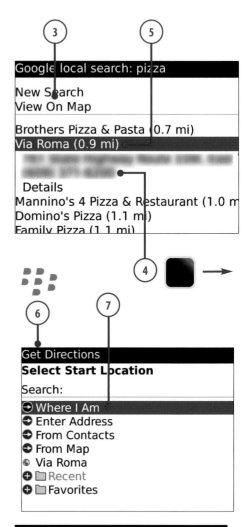

9. You then see a screen that enables you to modify the parameters of the route calculation. You can choose the Fastest Route or the Shortest Route. You can also select whether you want to Avoid Highways or Tolls.

10. Click Search to display the directions.

11. To see the directions on the map, click View On Map.

12. You will also see the route highlighted on the map.

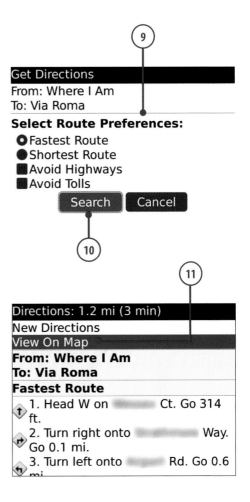

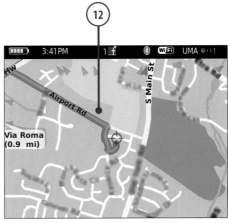

13. To start the GPS Navigation, press Menu, and choose Start GPS Navigation.

14. This guides you to your destination. At the bottom of the map, you see your speed, direction, and the number of satellites that the BlackBerry Curve's internal GPS or the external GPS can see.

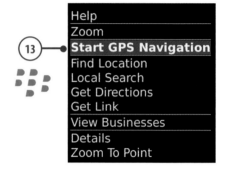

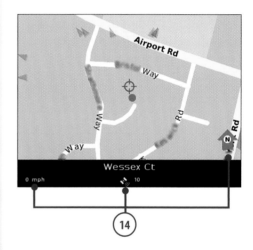

In this chapter, you learn how to use your BlackBerry Curve to keep in touch with your friends using Instant Messaging applications such as AIM and Google Talk and Social Networking applications such as Facebook and Twitter. Topics include the following:

→ Installing IM and social networking applications
→ Updating your status
→ Uploading pictures
→ Chatting with friends
→ BlackBerry Messenger

10

Social Networking and Instant Messaging on Your BlackBerry Curve

Instant Messaging applications such as AOL Instant Messenger, Google Talk, and ICQ have been popular for a long time now. Social Networking sites are fairly new but extremely popular. With your BlackBerry Curve, you can log in to your Facebook account to see what your friends are doing, upload pictures, and update your status. You can tweet about what you are up to on Twitter, and you can IM your buddies in real time. Your BlackBerry Curve also has a special IM application called BlackBerry Messenger that enables you to become friends with anyone in the world who has a BlackBerry.

Instant Messaging

Let's start with Instant Messaging (IM). Previously in Chapter 9, "Working with BlackBerry Applications," you learned how to find and install applications using BlackBerry App World. In this chapter, you will find all the IM clients for the BlackBerry Curve.

>>>*step-by-step*

IM Applications

Begin working with IM applications by going to BlackBerry App World.

1. You can find all your favorite IM applications in BlackBerry App World.

2. After you download one or more IM applications, you can find them in the Instant Messaging Folder on your BlackBerry Home Screen.

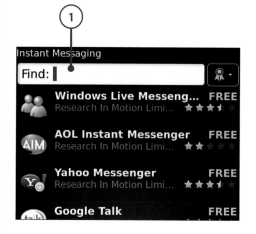

3. When you first run an IM application, you need to provide your login information.

4. Under the Sign In button, you can choose whether you want your BlackBerry to remember your login information, sign in automatically, or sign in as invisible.

5. All IM applications offer the same options. To configure your IM application, after you log in, press the Menu and choose Options.

6. Under Contacts, you can see Show Offline Contacts. The options are Yes, No, and Group. When you choose Group, your contacts will appear under separate headings making them easier to find.

7. Show Blocked Contacts enables you to choose whether to show or hide contacts that you blocked.

8. Show Display Pictures enables you to set whether to display or hide your contact's display pictures.

9. Under Conversations, you can see Save Message History. This enables you to save your conversations.

10. Show Conversations in Message List enables you to display your conversations with people in the BlackBerry's Messages application.

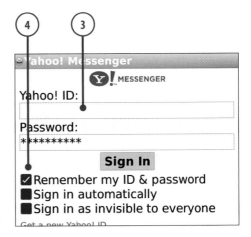

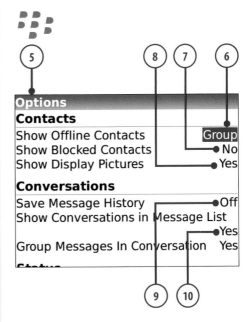

>>>*step-by-step*

Using IM to Chat

After you configure how you want your IM application to work, it's time to chat.

1. To chat with someone, scroll to his or her name, and click the trackball or trackpad.

2. While in a conversation, you can either type out smiling faces like :-) or press Symbol and choose them from the list. Depending on the IM application you use, there will be more or less emoticons available.

3. To send someone a file, press Menu, and choose Send File.

4. On the next screen, you need to choose what kind of file it is, or if it is not listed on the screen, choose File.

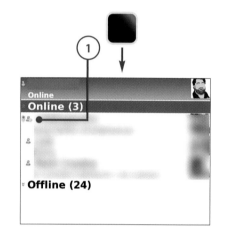

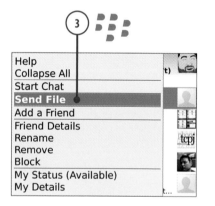

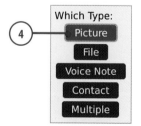

5. Use the trackball or trackpad to navigate to the file you want to send and click.

No IM Applications?

If you have a corporate BlackBerry, unfortunately your company can block IM applications. If you try to run any IM application, you see a message stating that it is disabled.

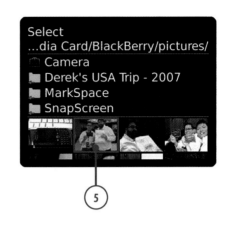

>>>step-by-step

BlackBerry Messenger

BlackBerry messenger is a special IM application designed specifically for BlackBerry users. If you know someone's BlackBerry PIN, no matter where in the world they are, you can add them to your BlackBerry Messenger contacts. You can also add people using their email addresses, but they do need to have a BlackBerry.

BlackBerry Messenger is special because it uses the BlackBerry network to communicate, which means it is always on and always available.

1. To open BlackBerry Messenger, click the icon in the Instant Messaging folder.

2. If it is the first time you are using BlackBerry Messenger, you are asked to type in your name. After you do this, you can see your contact list.

3. To configure BlackBerry Messenger, press Menu, and choose Options.

4. Vibrate When Receiving a Ping determines whether your BlackBerry Curve vibrates when someone pings you.

5. Ask Password Question When Adding Contacts determines whether people you add to your BlackBerry Messenger contacts must first type in a password to be added.

6. Allow Forwarding of Requests configures whether your requests to add someone to your contacts can be forwarded to another email address or BlackBerry. Set this to No to ensure that when you invite someone, the response you get is from that person and not someone else he might have forwarded your request to.

7. Show Conversations in Message List controls whether conversations you have with your BlackBerry Messenger contacts show in the main BlackBerry Messages application.

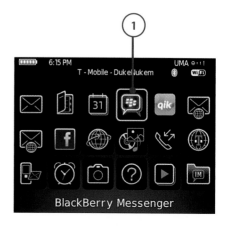

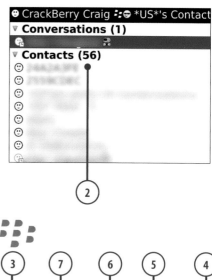

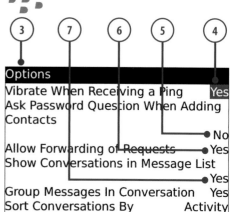

8. Consecutive messages that you send and receive are normally grouped together in a conversation. Set Group Messages in Conversation to No to stop this from happening.

9. Sort Conversations By changes the way that conversations are sorted. By default it is by activity, which means that the more recent conversation is at the top.

10. Press Enter Key to Send controls whether you can press Enter to send what you have typed. If you set this to No, you can press Enter to start a new line as you type. You need to click Send to send your text if you have this set to No.

11. Allow On the Phone Presence Status can be set to Yes or No. This controls whether BlackBerry Messenger automatically changes your status to reflect when you are on a phone call.

12. Allow Now Playing Presence Status controls whether you want BlackBerry Messenger to change your status to reflect the current song that you are listening to on your BlackBerry Curve.

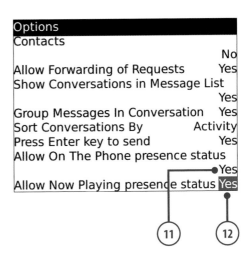

>>>*step-by-step*

Using BlackBerry Messenger

Like other IM applications, during a conversation with someone, you can send files and take other actions.

1. **Invite to Conference** enables you to invite more than one contact to a conference chat.

2. **Send a File** enables you to send a file to the contact.

3. **Send Voice Note** enables you to send a voice note that you recorded earlier to the contact.

4. **Send My Location** enables you to send your current location to the contact. The location is determined from the internal or external GPS.

5. **Ping Contact** enables you to send a ping to a contact. Sending a ping is a way to nudge the person to respond to you.

6. At any time, you can change your BlackBerry Messenger status by pressing Menu and choosing My Status.

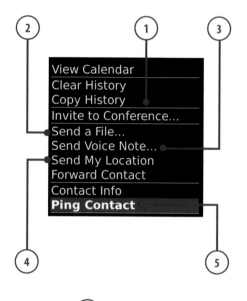

Social Networking

Social networking sites such as Facebook, MySpace, and Twitter are popular and enable more of us to keep in touch more often. Using these sites doesn't stop when you are on the road because your BlackBerry Curve has social networking applications.

If you look in the Social Networking category on BlackBerry App World, you see a list of social networking applications. Download the ones you are interested in.

Facebook

Let's take a look at Facebook. Before running the Facebook for BlackBerry application, you must already have a Facebook account. If you do not, visit http://www.facebook.com from a desktop computer and sign up for one.

>>>*step-by-step*

1. When you run the Facebook application for the first time, you see the Facebook Setup Wizard. It is important to pay close attention to this screen before continuing, especially the options under the Connect your Facebook account with section.

2. If you check the BlackBerry Message application option, it means that while you use BlackBerry Messenger and you receive an update in Facebook, the Facebook application can alert you of the update in real time.

3. If you check the BlackBerry Calendar application box, anytime you accept a meeting in Facebook, it is placed in your BlackBerry calendar.

4. If you select the BlackBerry Contacts application check box, the BlackBerry Facebook application looks through your entire BlackBerry address book to see if anyone is on Facebook.

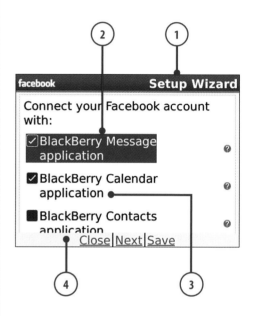

Be Wary of This Feature

If a match is found, a friend request is sent. Contact pictures are updated based on your friend's profile pictures if he or she is also in your BlackBerry address book. This also synchronizes your Facebook friend's birthday and contact information with her contact in your BlackBerry address book.

If you use your BlackBerry for business, it is probably not a good idea to check this box.

5. You need to select the email address that your Facebook update notifications go to. You also need to ensure that you allow email updates to be sent in Facebook. When you finish, click Save.

>>>step-by-step

Configuring Facebook

Before you start using Facebook, let's configure it first.

1. Press Menu, and choose Options. The top half of the Options screen is the same as the Setup Wizard screen, and you can make changes to the selections you made earlier if you want to.

   If you scroll down to the bottom of the Options screen, you see some extra settings.

2. **Leave email notification messages on mail server** sets whether your BlackBerry leaves the Facebook notification emails on the email server, or deletes them when it has taken note of the update.

3. The **Prompt before refreshing friend list** controls whether you want to be prompted before your BlackBerry refreshes your list of Facebook friends.

4. **Check spelling before sending** controls whether you want the Facebook application to check your spelling before it posts any updates you write.

5. If **Automatically check for the newest version of Facebook** is checked, your BlackBerry looks for newer versions of Facebook and offers to upgrade.

6. **Clear Cache** allows you to clear the Facebook cache. The Facebook application keeps a lot of information in a local cache so that it can quickly update the screen. If you are running low on memory, clearing this cache can help.

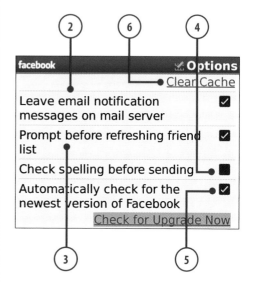

>>>*step-by-step*

Using Facebook

Let's take a look at the Facebook main screen.

1. You can type your status updates right on the main screen.

2. Highlights of your friend's status updates are below.

   Along the top of the screen is a list of icons.

3. View Status Updates takes you to the main Facebook screen. Instead of scrolling to this icon in the future, you can also press the S key to jump to it directly.

4. Notifications displays your notifications and your friend's notifications. Instead of scrolling to this icon in the future, you can also press the N key to jump to it directly.

5. Upload a Photo enables you to upload a photo to one of your Facebook photo albums. Instead of scrolling to this icon in the future, you can also press the U key to jump to it directly.

6. When you click the camera icon, you see a list of all the photos on your BlackBerry Curve. You can either select one of them, or click Camera to take a photo in real time.

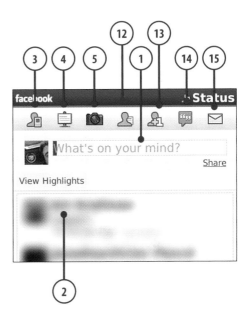

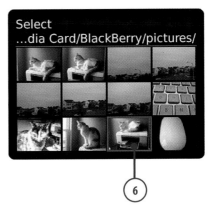

7. On the next screen, you can write a photo caption.

8. Choose which Facebook album the photo must be uploaded to.

9. If you want to tag the photo, click Tag This Photo.

10. When you choose to tag a photo, you can move the box to the appropriate person and click the trackball or trackpad to select the person.

11. Next type in the person who is in the photo. As you type, your friends appear in a drop-down list.

12. The Friends icon shows all your Facebook friends. When you click a friend, you can view his profile, write on his wall, poke him, or send him a message. You can press the F key to jump to it directly.

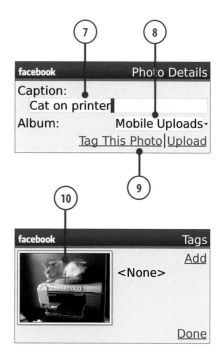

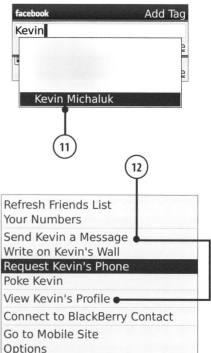

13. The Add a Friend icon enables you to add a friend. You can type in his or her email address and an optional message. You can press the J key to jump to it directly.

14. The Wall icon enables you to write on someone's wall. When you click this icon, you can type your friend's name in. As you type, the BlackBerry filters a drop-down list. You can press the W key to jump to it directly.

15. The Message icon enables you to send a message to one of your friends. You can press the M key to jump to it directly.

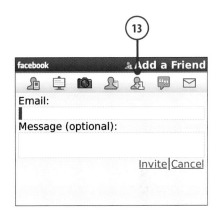

>>>*step-by-step*

Twitter

Let's take a look at Twitter next. Oddly there is no Twitter application in the BlackBerry App World, but you can find great BlackBerry Twitter clients on other sites. One such client is ÜberTwitter. To download ÜberTwitter OTA, use the BlackBerry browser, and go to http://www.ubertwitter.com/bb/download.php.

When ÜberTwitter is installed, run it. You can usually find it in the Downloads folder on the BlackBerry Home Screen.

Before your use ÜberTwitter or any Twitter application, you must have a Twitter account. Go to http://www.twitter.com to sign up for one.

1. On the main ÜberTwitter screen, you see the tweets of people you are following.

2. If you click someone's tweet, you can see the entire tweet. If you click again, you can Reply, Reply All, ReTweet, or Direct Message.

3. To update your own status (in other words tweet), press Menu, and choose Update My Status.

4. If you want to add a picture to your tweet, click the trackball or trackpad, and choose Take Picture. You then can take a picture with your BlackBerry Curve's camera.

5. To see who is following you on Twitter, press Menu, and choose My Followers.

6. To see Twitter users near you, press Menu, and choose Everyone Near You.

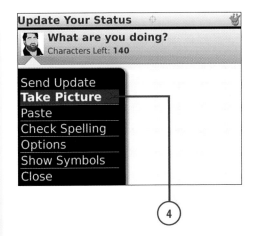

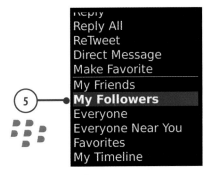

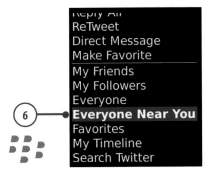

>>>step-by-step

QIK

Another popular application in the social category is QIK. QIK enables you to upload or stream videos directly from your BlackBerry Curve. Like most applications, you find QIK in BlackBerry App World.

Before you use QIK on your BlackBerry, sign up for an account at http://www.qik.com.

1. After you log in to QIK, press Menu, and choose Settings.

2. Video Camera Integration has three choices. This controls what QIK does with videos that you record using QIK. You can automatically upload them to your QIK account, ask before uploading, or never upload (Off).

3. Location Privacy controls if the video you record contains your GPS coordinates, and if it does, how accurate it is. Your choices are Off, City Level, Street Level, and Precisely.

4. Connectivity controls how QIK connects to the QIK servers to upload your videos. If available, it is best to choose Wi-Fi. It is free and it is the fastest choice. Use 3G Network enables you to use your cellular carrier's network.

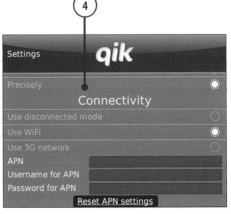

>>>*step-by-step*

Using QIK

Now you are ready to use QIK.

1. Before you start, type in a title and description of the video.

2. Select whether the video is public or private.

3. Select whether the audio is muted.

4. Click the red button to start recording the video. When you stop recording, the video uploads to your QIK page.

5. If you want to stream a video in real time, press Menu, and choose Start Streaming. As you record a video, it is streamed to your QIK page for others to watch.

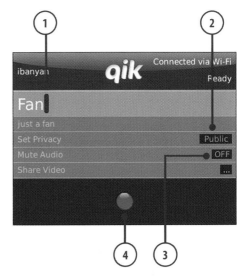

In this chapter, you learn how to customize your BlackBerry Curve. Customization includes using themes that completely transform the look and feel of your BlackBerry Curve, to selecting a background wallpaper, to moving your icons around. Topics include the following:

→ Downloading and using BlackBerry themes
→ Setting your wallpaper
→ Moving applications and using folders
→ Changing fonts
→ Customizing the convenience buttons

11

Customizing Your BlackBerry Curve

Your BlackBerry Curve looks great and functions seamlessly. But what if you get bored with how it looks? You can customize the look and feel of your BlackBerry Curve and breathe some new life into it. Everything will still function the same, but it will look like a new BlackBerry. You can make simple changes like changing the wallpaper or fonts, or just rearrange your icons.

BlackBerry Themes

Using BlackBerry themes is the best way to customize your BlackBerry Curve. A theme can change everything about the look and feel of your BlackBerry Curve, including the fonts, the colors of text, the colors of menus, the look of menus, the icons on the Home screen, the top row indicators, and the look of the Today screen.

Unfortunately, BlackBerry themes are not sold in the BlackBerry App World. However, they are easy to find. Here are some places where you can download free BlackBerry themes or purchase them:

- **bplay**. http://www.bplay.com/themes

- **BlackBerry Themes**. http://www.blackberrythemes.net/

- **CrackBerry.com**. http://crackberry.com/download/themes

- **Themes4BB**. http://www.themes4bb.com/

- **Elecite**. http://www.elecite.com/

All these websites can be accessed using your BlackBerry's browser. However, you also can browse and purchase the themes using your desktop computer and have the download link emailed or SMSed to your BlackBerry. Downloading and installing a BlackBerry theme is the same as downloading and installing a regular BlackBerry application. The exception being that many themes require that you pull out your BlackBerry Curve's battery after they are installed. If this is not done, they will be unavailable.

There are three kinds of BlackBerry themes:

- **Zen**. With this style of theme, the BlackBerry Today Screen has a row of icons at the bottom. These icons are the same ones that are in the top row when you view your Home Screen.

- **Today**. With this style of theme, your most recent three to five emails are listed on the screen, along with your upcoming appointments.

- **Today Plus (Today +)**. This type of theme is a combination of the Zen and Today themes.

Once you have installed a new theme and pulled the battery if required, the following steps show you how to use that theme.

Beware of the Version

Always make sure that the theme you want to buy or download is written for your BlackBerry Curve's software version. If you download a theme that is not 100% compatible with your BlackBerry's software version, your BlackBerry Curve could start acting up and even become unusable.

>>>*step-by-step*

Changing Your Theme

These steps show you how to change your BlackBerry Theme.

1. Click Settings.

2. Click Options.

3. Scroll down to Theme, and click.

4. You see all the themes you have installed. As you scroll over each theme, you see a preview.

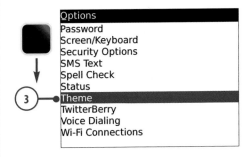

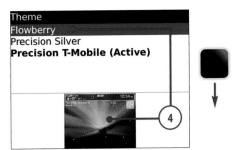

5. Click a theme to use it. When you first switch themes, your BlackBerry takes a few seconds to make all the changes.

Theme Change Lag

After you switch themes, you may notice a slight lag the first time you open the Home and Today screens. After that, things will return to normal.

Your BlackBerry Curve now has a totally new look!

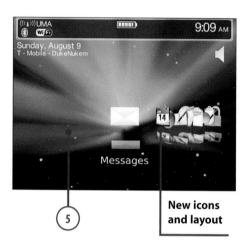

New icons and layout

New icons **New Home Screen**

>>>step-by-step

Changing Your Font

If you want a small change in how your BlackBerry Curve looks, or if you feel like you need larger or clearer text, changing the font can be useful.

1. From the BlackBerry Home Screen, click Settings.

2. From the Settings folder, click Options.

3. From the Options screen, click Screen/Keyboard.

4. The Screen/Keyboard Options screen allows you to change the Font Family, Font Size, and Font Style.

5. Click the name of the Font Family to select a different Font Family.

6. As you scroll through each font, you see an example of what it looks like.

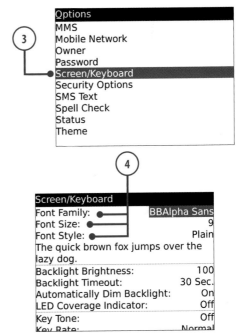

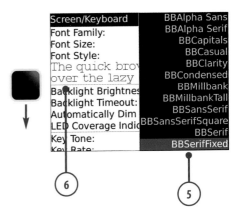

7. After you have selected a new font, you can change the Font Size.

8. Next, you can change the Font Style.

9. Font Smoothing is a useful option if you are finding it hard to read text on your BlackBerry Curve. On liquid crystal displays (LCDs) like the ones used in the BlackBerry Curve, some text can look pixilated.

10. If you turn on Font Smoothing, your BlackBerry Curve smoothes out the curves and edges of the text, making it easier to read.

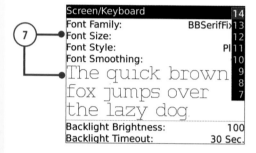

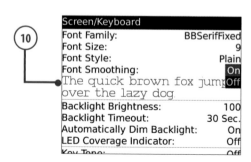

While we are on the Screen/Keyboard Options screen, if you scroll down, you see an option for the Currency Key. This allows you to change the Currency Key on your BlackBerry Curve's keyboard. On U.S. BlackBerry keyboards, the key is to a U.S. dollar, and the key has a dollar symbol on it. If you need to change which symbol is produced when you click the Currency Key, change it here.

Click to change currency symbol

Screen/Keyboard	
Font Style:	Plain
The quick brown fox jumps over the lazy dog.	
Backlight Brightness:	100
Backlight Timeout:	30 Sec.
Automatically Dim Backlight:	On
LED Coverage Indicator:	Off
Key Tone:	O
Key Rate:	Norm
Currency Key:	
Right Side Convenience Key Opens:	

Before we close this Options screen, scroll down a bit further, and you see a place to change the BlackBerry's convenience keys. These are the keys on the left and right of your BlackBerry Curve. By default, the left convenience key is used for voice dialing. (If you use a BlackBerry Curve 8350i, it is used for PTT.) The Right Convenience key is used for the camera by default.

You can change these keys to run any application installed on your BlackBerry Curve. If you need a quick way to get to your Facebook fix, change the Left Convenience key to run Facebook.

Click to change application

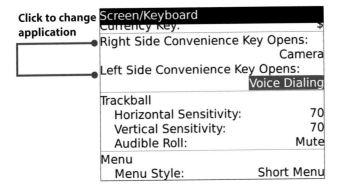

Screen/Keyboard	
Currency Key:	$
Right Side Convenience Key Opens:	Camera
Left Side Convenience Key Opens:	Voice Dialing
Trackball	
Horizontal Sensitivity:	70
Vertical Sensitivity:	70
Audible Roll:	Mute
Menu	
Menu Style:	Short Menu

>>>step-by-step

Changing the Home Screen Image (Wallpaper)

Another small change that you can make that customizes your BlackBerry Curve is to change the Home Screen image. This is sometimes called the Wallpaper.

1. While viewing a picture in the Media Player, press the Menu key and choose Set As Home Screen Image.

2. If you change your mind, you can reset the Home Screen image to the default picture used in the theme you are using. Return to any picture, press the Menu key, and choose Reset Home Screen Image.

3. When you return to the Home Screen, you will see the new image.

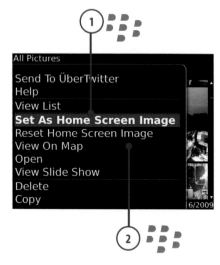

Rearranging Your Applications

Your BlackBerry Curve allows you to move applications around and move them in and out of folders, which helps you organize them better.

1. To move an application, scroll to that application's icon, press the Menu key, and choose Move.

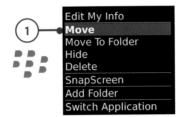

2. Four-way arrows appear around the application's icon. Use the trackball or trackpad to move the icon to its new position. Click the trackball or trackpad to release the icon at its new position.

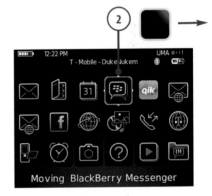

3. To move an application to a folder, scroll to the application. You may want to move an application from a folder to the Home Screen, also called the Home folder, for quicker access. Press the Menu key and choose Move To Folder.

4. Select the folder to move the application to. If you want the application on the Home Screen, choose Home.

5. If you want to add a new folder to your Home Screen, first scroll to an existing folder. Press the Menu key and choose Add Folder.

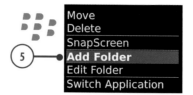

6. Give your folder a name, choose the icon it will use, and click Add.

7. Your new folder appears on the Home Screen.

8. To edit one of your folders or an existing folder, scroll to the folder, click the Menu key, and choose Edit Folder.

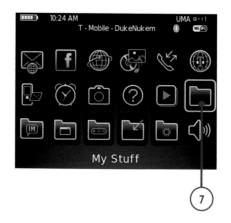

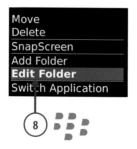

Securing Your BlackBerry Curve

You can secure your BlackBerry Curve so that if someone picks it up, that person can't access your information. To do this, you can set a password.

>>>*step-by-step*

1. From the Settings screen, select Options, Password.

2. Change Password to Enabled, and click the Set Password button.

3. Type in the password you want to use.

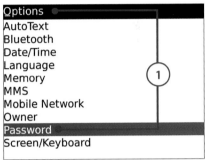

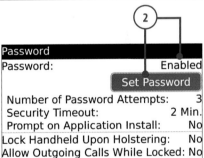

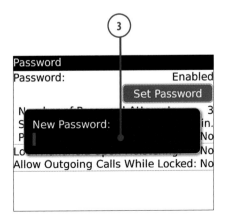

4. Verify your password.

   Before you exit this screen, it is very important to pay attention to the other password settings.

5. Number of Password Attempts is set to 3. This controls how many times you can type your password incorrectly before your BlackBerry Curve erases all its data.

Password Trouble

If you have trouble entering your password, make sure that your BlackBerry Curve is not in caps lock or num lock mode.

6. Security Timeout controls how long your BlackBerry Curve waits before locking the screen and requiring you to enter your password again. A higher number is less annoying, but if you are worried about someone stealing your BlackBerry, a lower number is better, because it gives the thief less time.

7. Set Prompt on Application Install to Yes to require your password to be entered every time you install a new application.

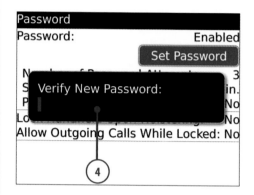

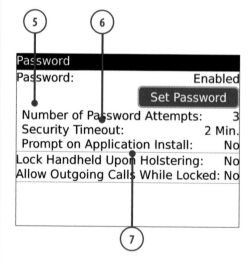

8. Set Lock Handheld Upon Holstering to Yes if you want your BlackBerry Curve to lock when you put it in its holster or case.

9. Set Allow Outgoing Calls While Locked to Yes to allow someone to make outgoing calls even though your BlackBerry is locked. If someone steals your BlackBerry, this would allow the thief to make phone calls, so it is advisable to leave it set to No.

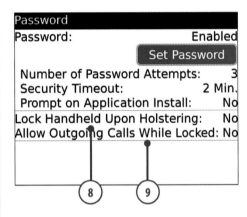

Setting Airplane Mode

When you fly, you are always required to turn off your phone. Of course, you can do so many things with your BlackBerry that you probably want to leave it turned on. The compromise is to turn off all the radios. This satisfies the airlines and allows you to watch videos, catch up on emails, and listen to music during your flight.

>>>step-by-step

1. To turn off all radios, click Manage Connections on the BlackBerry Home Screen.

2. Click Turn All Connections Off.

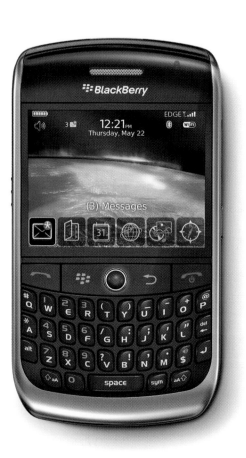

In this chapter, you learn how to maintain your BlackBerry Curve and the BlackBerry software on your computer. Topics include the following:

→ Managing your BlackBerry Curve's memory
→ Updating your BlackBerry Curve's software
→ Resetting and restarting your BlackBerry Curve
→ Keeping your BlackBerry Curve clean

Maintaining Your BlackBerry Curve and Solving Problems

As you spend more time with your BlackBerry Curve, you will want to keep it in tip-top shape and always up to date with the latest software. We cover how to do just that.

Extending Battery Life

Your BlackBerry already does a great job of running for a long time on a single charge, but there are ways of improving that battery life.

>>>step-by-step

The first way to extend battery life is to make your BlackBerry turn itself on and off. Because you probably don't need to use your BlackBerry overnight, having it turn itself off and on conserves all the battery power that would be used overnight.

1. Click Settings on the BlackBerry Home Screen.

2. Click Options from the Settings folder.

3. On the Options screen, click on Auto On/Off.

   Use the Auto On/Off screen to configure when your BlackBerry should turn on and turn off.

   The screen is broken into two sections. The top section is for setting Auto On/Off on weekdays. The bottom section is for setting Auto On/Off on the weekend.

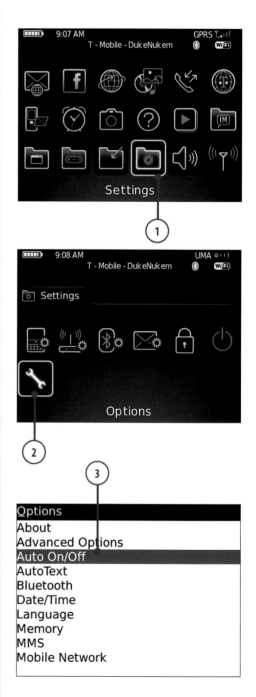

4. Change Weekday to Enabled.

5. Change Turn On At to the time you need your BlackBerry to turn itself on.

6. Set Turn Off At to the time you need your BlackBerry to turn itself off.

7. If you want your BlackBerry to remain turned off over the weekend, leave Weekend set to Disabled. This is typically true if you use your BlackBerry for work and don't need it over the weekend.

   If you need your BlackBerry over the weekend, set Weekend to Enabled.

8. Set Turn On At to the time you need your BlackBerry to turn itself on.

9. Set Turn Off At to the time you need your BlackBerry to turn itself off.

10. Press the Escape button and choose Save to save your changes.

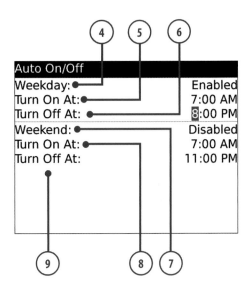

Note

If your BlackBerry has turned off automatically, to turn it on prematurely, press the red call end button, which is also the power button.

>>>*step-by-step*

Turn Your Radio Off in Low Signal Areas

The next way to extend your battery life is to turn off your BlackBerry's cellular radio if you are in very low or no-signal areas for long periods of time.

1. Click Manage Connections from the BlackBerry Home Screen.

2. Uncheck the box next to Mobile Network.

3. When you return to coverage, remember to return to this screen and put back the check next to Mobile Network.

>>>*step-by-step*

Turn Off Bluetooth

Another way to extend the battery life on your BlackBerry Curve is to turn off Bluetooth when you are not using it. With Bluetooth headsets in heavy use, this is not always possible, because you never know when you'll need to answer an incoming call. However, at night you should turn off Bluetooth, especially if you do not use the Auto On/Off feature.

1. Click Manage Connections from the BlackBerry Home Screen.

2. Uncheck the box next to Bluetooth.

3. Return to this screen to enable Bluetooth when you need to.

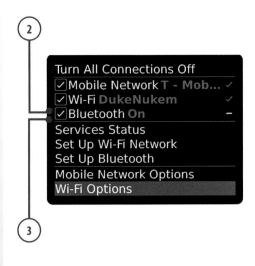

The type of applications you use on your BlackBerry can affect battery life. The more CPU-intensive the application is, or the more it downloads or uploads data to the cellular network, the more battery power it uses.

If you can, close applications you are not using that you think are consuming a lot of battery power.

Keeping Your BlackBerry Curve Clean and Safe

Because a BlackBerry is handled frequently, oil from your hands can leave smudges on the screen. To keep your BlackBerry Curve's screen clean, rub it with a microfiber cloth or pad specifically designed for phone screens.

Because the BlackBerry Curve's screen is plastic, do not use any fabric that might scratch it. A scratched screen is hard to fix. Never use chemicals to clean the BlackBerry's screen, either. A damp cloth will do the trick.

Note

Keys, coins, and BlackBerrys do not mix. If you do not use a BlackBerry holster, be conscious of which pocket you put your BlackBerry in. Keys and coins are metal and will scratch the screen and case. Occasionally keys can damage the USB port on the BlackBerry, which may require you to purchase a new one.

Keeping Your BlackBerry Curve Up to Date

Many new features are added when RIM releases new software for your BlackBerry Curve. There are two ways to update your BlackBerry Curve's software.

>>>*step-by-step*

Updating Over the Air (OTA)

1. Click Settings on the BlackBerry Home Screen.

2. From the Settings folder, click Options.

3. On the Options screen, click Advanced Options.

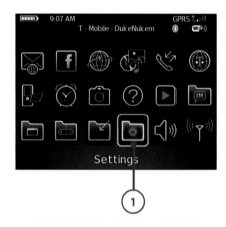

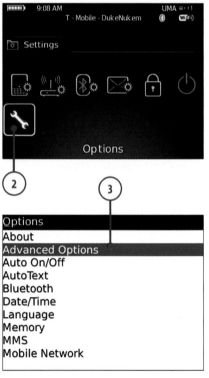

4. On the Advanced Options screen, click Wireless Upgrade.

5. The Wireless Upgrade screen shows which version you are running and lists any new versions you can upgrade to.

   If you want to check for an update manually, click Check for Upgrades.

6. If you see a new update for your BlackBerry Curve, press the Menu key and choose Start Download.

7. Follow the instructions to download and install the new update.

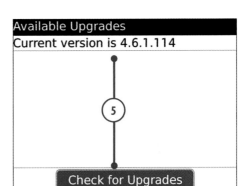

>>>step-by-step

Updating with BlackBerry Desktop Manager

If you don't want to wait for your BlackBerry Curve to update over the air, or if your wireless carrier doesn't support wireless updates, you can use the BlackBerry Desktop Manager. Unfortunately, if you have an Apple Macintosh, there is currently no way to update using PocketMac for BlackBerry. However, in the near future RIM will release BlackBerry Desktop Manager for Mac, which will support this feature.

Very often when you run BlackBerry Desktop Manager each day, it checks to see if any updates are available and prompts you to install them. Follow these steps:

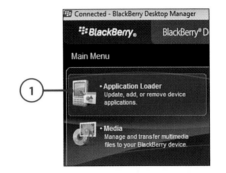

1. Connect your BlackBerry Curve to your PC using the USB cable, and run BlackBerry Desktop Manager. Click Application Loader.

2. On the next screen, click Start, located under Update Software.

3. The BlackBerry Desktop Manager reads your BlackBerry's configuration.

4. Select the version of software you want to upgrade your BlackBerry to, and click Next.

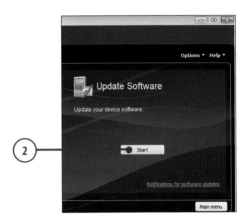

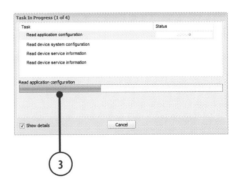

5. The next screen shows an update summary.

Note

BlackBerry Desktop Manager automatically backs up all the data on your BlackBerry before the update. It restores the data after the update so that there is no danger of losing anything.

6. One last summary screen appears. Click Finish.

7. Your BlackBerry is updated. This can take up to an hour, depending on how many contacts, calendar entries, emails, and applications you have on your BlackBerry.

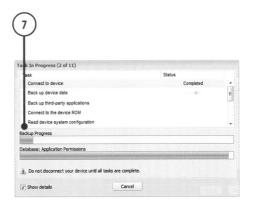

Solving BlackBerry Curve Problems

Occasionally your BlackBerry Curve will start acting up—running slowly, not receiving emails, or not connecting to the cellular network properly. Here are a few things your can do to try to solve the problem before calling tech support.

Soft-Reset Your BlackBerry

Press and release the Alt, Right-Shift, and Delete keys at the same time. This performs a soft reset.

Alt

Delete

Right-Shift

Hard-Reset Your BlackBerry

A hard reset is a great way to release memory that is being used by an application that has a memory leak.

To hard-reset your BlackBerry, pull out the battery, wait for 15 seconds, and reinsert it.

Because this is a hard reset, your BlackBerry will take longer to reboot.

Cycle the Radios

If your BlackBerry is not connecting to the network correctly, or it seems to not be receiving emails, SMSs, or PINs, try a radio cycle.

1. Click Manage Connections.

2. Click Turn All Connections Off. All radios go off. When they do, Turn All Connections Off changes to Turn All Connections On.

3. To turn on the radios, click Turn All Connections On.

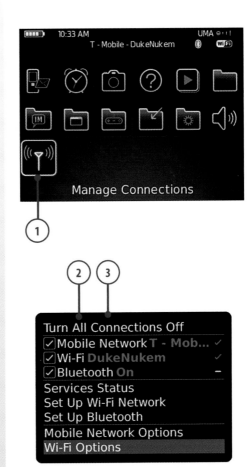

Wipe Your BlackBerry

If you want to return your BlackBerry to its factory settings and delete all your data, you can do a wipe. You normally do this if you are giving your BlackBerry to someone else. When you perform a wipe, the data on your media card does not get wiped.

If you want to use your BlackBerry Curve after you have wiped it, be sure you back it up using the BlackBerry Desktop Manager first.

Performing a Wipe

1. Click Settings on the BlackBerry Home Screen.

2. Click Options on the Settings folder.

3. On the Options screen, click Security Options.

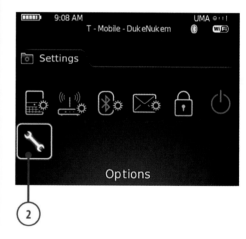

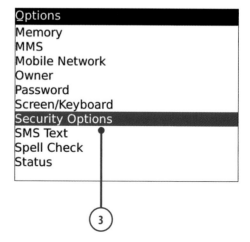

4. On the Security Options screen, click General Settings.

5. Press the Menu button, and choose Wipe Handheld.

6. Click Continue.

7. You are prompted to type **blackberry** to confirm the wipe. Once you enter blackberry, your BlackBerry is now wiped.

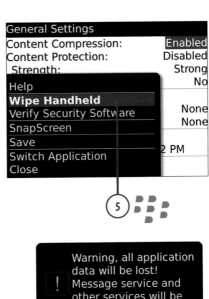

Don't Run Out of Memory

If your BlackBerry runs out of memory or runs very low on memory, it will start running very slowly. In addition, it will start deleting old emails and calendar entries to free up memory.

If your BlackBerry Curve starts running slowly, check to see how much memory it has available.

>>>*step-by-step*

1. Press and release the Alt, Right-Shift, and H keys at the same time.

2. You see the BlackBerry Help Me! Screen.

3. Scroll to the bottom, and you see File Free. This number should be well above 200000 Bytes (which is 200KB). If it is below 200KB, your BlackBerry Curve is most likely running slowly and deleting old emails.

Alt   **Right-Shift**

2

Help Me!
BlackBerry
By Research In Motion Limited.

If you are having problems, please call technical support.

Vendor ID:	100
Platform:	4.2.0.76
App Version:	4.6.1.114 (185)
PIN:	208a5418
IMEI:	004401.13.050181.6
MAC:	00:23:7a:ce:10:d9

3

Help Me!
Vendor ID:	100
Platform:	4.2.0.76
App Version:	4.6.1.114 (185)
PIN:	208a5418
IMEI:	004401.13.050181.6
MAC:	00:23:7a:ce:10:d9
Uptime:	165399 secs
Signal Strength:	-85 dBm
Battery Level:	50%
File Free:	99591981 Bytes
File Total:	207749120 Bytes

To rectify a BlackBerry Curve that has run out of memory, perform a hard reset, as discussed earlier. If your BlackBerry is still out of memory after a hard reset, you need to start removing applications and deleting old emails. If you do not have a media card in your BlackBerry Curve, you may need to delete pictures.

If you do not have a media card, and your BlackBerry Curve is running out of memory, it would be a good idea to buy one.

Getting Help with Your BlackBerry Curve

If you are still having problems with your BlackBerry Curve, there are many places you can turn to:

- **The BlackBerry website.** Visit the BlackBerry website at http://www.BlackBerry.com. After you select your country, click Support and Services, and then click Smartphone Support.

- **Your wireless carrier's website.** Your local wireless carrier will offer support for your BlackBerry Curve.

- **BlackBerry Community websites.** The BlackBerry Community is very strong and active on the Internet. You can find help with your BlackBerry Curve issues by asking questions in the forums. Here are some of the more popular sites:

  - **CrackBerry.com.** http://www.crackberry.com/

  - **Pinstack.com.** http://pinstack.com/

  - **BlackBerryForums.** http://www.blackberryforums.com/

  - **BlackBerry Support Community Forums.** http://supportforums.blackberry.com/rim/

- **Me.** I would be happy to answer your questions. Visit http://www.MyBlackBerryCurve.info and leave a question or send me an email.

Index

Like this book? Check out other titles in this series.

ISBN: 9780789742391

Brad Miser

My iPod touch®

My iPod touch provides expert advice and easy to follow, full-color tasks with ample illustrations to get your iPod rockin' in no time.

ISBN: 9780789742315

Brad Miser

My iPhone™, 3rd Edition

The 3rd edition shows you how to use Apple's newest addition to the iPhone family, the 3GS. Quick, easy to follow tasks—in full color! Covers both the 3S and 3GS.

Coming Soon:
My Palm Pre and My MacBook

que®

These books are available at retailers everywhere or informit.com/que.